Spark Change

MAKING YOUR MARK
IN A DIGITAL WORLD

Olivia Van Ledtje and Cynthia Merrill

International Society for Technology in Education

PORTLAND, OREGON • ARLINGTON, VIRGINIA

Spark Change
Making Your Mark in a Digital World
Olivia Van Ledtje and Cynthia Merrill

© 2019 International Society for Technology in Education
World rights reserved. No part of this book may be reproduced or transmitted in
any form or by any means—electronic, mechanical, photocopying, recording, or by
any information storage or retrieval system—without prior written permission from
the publisher. Contact Permission Editor: iste.org/about/permissions-and-reprints;
permissions@iste.org; fax: 1.541.302.3780.

Senior Acquisitions Editor: *Valerie Witte*
Copy Editor: *Linda Laflamme*
Proofreader: *Kate Bradley*
Indexer: *Valerie Haynes Perry*
Book Design and Production: *Mayfly Design*
Cover Design: *Edwin Ouellette*

Library of Congress Cataloging-in-Publication Data Available

First Edition
ISBN: 978-1-56484-786-7
Ebook version available
Printed in the United States of America
ISTE® is a registered trademark of the International Society for Technology in
Education

About ISTE

The International Society for Technology in Education (ISTE) is a nonprofit organization that works with the global education community to accelerate the use of technology to solve tough problems and inspire innovation. Our worldwide network believes in the potential technology holds to transform teaching and learning.

ISTE sets a bold vision for education transformation through the ISTE Standards, a framework for students, educators, administrators, coaches and computer science educators to rethink education and create innovative learning environments. ISTE hosts the annual ISTE Conference & Expo, one of the world's most influential edtech events. The organization's professional learning offerings include online courses, professional networks, year-round academies, peer-reviewed journals, and other publications. ISTE is also the leading publisher of books focused on technology in education. For more information or to become an ISTE member, visit iste.org. Subscribe to ISTE's YouTube channel and connect with ISTE on Twitter, Facebook, and LinkedIn.

Related ISTE Titles

Digital Citizenship in Action: Empowering Students to Engage in Online Communities
Kristen Mattson

Teach Boldly: Using Edtech for Social Good
Jennifer Williams

To see all books available from ISTE, please visit iste.org/books.

About the Authors

Olivia Van Ledtje ("LivBit") is a reader, thinker, and kids' voice believer. Using technology to inspire empathy, equity, and activism, Olivia's mission is to share messages with the world that are hopeful, kind, and true. Olivia is the creator of LivBits—short videos for kids and teachers about reading, thinking, and life. Her work is featured internationally as a model for digital citizenship and kid creation.

Cynthia Merrill is a consultant, speaker, and author dedicated to strengthening literacy and tech experiences for all students. She works in diverse school communities throughout the United States coaching, training, and encouraging administrators and teachers in their practices. Cynthia is passionate about creating authentic opportunities for students to document their thinking using tech tools.

Contents

Chapter Seven: Digital Future 97

Have you ever thought about the sparks needed to ignite the future for kids and technology?

Foreword

One of the very first lessons I learned when I was a new teacher with technology was to pay extra careful attention to how students were inventing new tools and achieving far beyond what the adults thought was even possible. Never underestimate the creativity of how young people imagine and invent. Olivia Van Ledtje's work is one of those examples in history of how a young mind with an endless passion for learning can apply technology in such an enlightening fashion as to lead to a breakthrough in thinking.

Olivia's writing, knowledge network, excitement for continuous learning, and global reach to solve problems with her use of Twitter combine to create aha moments. Lessons learned from Liv's experience of building a global reach from the time she was 9 years old (now 11) make her a veteran in the field. Her work upends the current thinking of a sense of protecting children by blocking them from social media to an urgency to teach all children how to leverage global networks to enrich their lives and make the world a better place.

I have had the pleasure of watching Liv's engagement with the world from the time she began her Twitter account. I joked with her that one day she might have 1,000 followers! I just slightly underestimated (she now has close to 50,000). Her sense of how to use Twitter to share her message of positive living for young people, to share her love of books (and sharks), and to reach out to people around the world has attracted a following of teachers, professors, authors, illustrators, parents, librarians, and more.

Recently, I called Liv to discuss some ideas for this foreword. I called during the school day thinking I would leave a voice mail and Liv would call me back. To my surprise, she answered the phone. I had to ask, "Are you in school?" Her response was "Yes." But I soon found out the school was 500 miles from her home in New Hampshire. She was in Ohio. "What are you doing in Ohio?" I asked. Liv replied, "I am here to open the dedication to the ukulele program for this elementary school." I was totally confused. Why would an 11-year-old travel 500 miles for the opening of a ukulele program? The reason turned out to make perfect sense. Through social media, Liv discovered that the school could only fund its highly successful ukulele program (for grades K–5) for a small part of the year because of budget issues. Liv's sense of social justice prompted her to immediately use her Twitter account to seek donations of ukuleles from around the world. At the time of my call, 32 ukuleles had been shipped to the school. That is the number the school needed to continue a year-long program. Problem identified. Problem solved. Go, Liv.

I would hope that there would be wide agreement that this was a productive use of Twitter. Liv made the world a slightly better place. There was no assignment from a teacher, no prodding from her parents. Liv simply activated her worldwide network that she had been building for years to solve the problem with her communication skills. However, I must share with you that I have invited Liv to present her use of Twitter at my summer conference, with mixed reviews.

While some educators have been thankful she was on the program to share her work, others criticized me for what they considered was an inappropriate use of social media by an underage student. I understand that social media is typically forbidden in schools. In my early years in teaching, word processors were also banned as a cheating tool for student writing.

My concern is that our caution to protect children from the negative consequences of young people using social media might prove to be a block to the incredible positive experiences that Liv has had. My sense is that by the time Liv graduates from high school, she will have solved many more real-world problems with her global network, expanded her vocabulary, deepened her appreciation of cultures around the world, and fed her passion for learning (currently sharks). Her research, writing, and organizational skills will be further honed. If no other student in her future high school has had her set of experiences, they will potentially be graduating with a significant disadvantage of applying their knowledge compared to what Liv can already do as an 11-year-old. This is really an equity issue.

Of course, Liv's work has been possible in part because she has the support of her mother, Cynthia Merrill, who empowers her to use social media and other tools to share her ideas online and in the "real world." This support is critical and is nowhere more evident than in this collaborative work. By working together on this book, Liv and Cynthia demonstrate what student voice and agency can look like when adults (parents and educators) recognize that children can use social media as a tool for learning and making the world a better place.

Please read this book with an open mind about the creativity and natural desire to learn that all children have. Social media is not going away soon; it has become a mainstream tool for our society. My fear is that if we do not teach students the appropriate use of these powerful tools, our worst fears of negative consequences will come true. Many students will use these tools without permission from their teachers or parents. This book inspires us to take the high moral and creative ground to prepare our students for success in the world they live. I am grateful to Liv and Cynthia for the time and thought they put into this book to share their stories with the world. Enjoy every page.

Alan November

Acknowledgments

Cynthia: This book would never have been possible without many incredible people encouraging me and Liv along the way. We'd like to give a special heartbeep shout-out to Maureen Emery; Ruth Van Ledtje; Cris Tovani; Matt Soeth; Nate Butkus and his amazing parents; Eric and Jennifer; Helen the Shark; Susan Bunch; Cara Newman; Kelly Hoenie; Alan November; our Upper Arlington, Ohio, fan club (Kristin and Sadie Bugnitz, Jill Merkle, and Shannon Hemmelgarn); and our New Jersey people (Diana DaCosta, Louie and Elliana DaCosta, Stephanie Teele Ross, and Dr. Joanne Pollara).

Deb Craig, colleague and friend to me, and quiet fierce supporter of Liv from the very beginning: Thank you for all the times you spoke after Liv in conference presentations and only mildly complained about it. Thank you for always sending the absolute perfect Bitmojis when I needed them most as I was writing this book. There isn't anyone else I'd want on this journey. You've seen our hard work first-hand, and you've held me up when I've needed it most. I'm so grateful to know you.

> **Liv:** Deb, I'm so happy you understand me, laugh with me, and listen to me! I hope this book makes you feel proud of all the stories we shared in our LivBit adventures. Also, thank you for always keeping most of my crazy and annoying habits a secret. I love you very much.

Cynthia: I could have never written this book without Anne Collier. Her incredible insight for how digital spaces have grown and changed in the past decade has been invaluable to me, but most importantly, her incredible encouragement early on helped me know this story mattered. Anne, thank you for always taking my call, answering my endless questions sent in long text threads, and being an incredible model for the kind of thinker I hope to be for this world.

> **Liv:** Anne, do you remember that time we had dinner together in NYC? I will never forget how genuine you were in your encouragement of me and Muma. Your eyes have so much love for the world and for me. Thank you for believing in us!

Cynthia: Pana Asavavatana has been an important colleague and believer in the work Liv and I do together since the very beginning. Pana, it's no surprise how quickly you moved from online interactions with both of my girls to a very special space in our hearts. Your encouragement of Liv (and Charlotte) never goes unnoticed, but in case I've never explicitly said how special your encouragement is, I want you to know that I could not have done any of this without you. Thank you for being such a true friend and loyal supporter of my work—but most importantly of my heart. Your quiet, consistent encouragement helped me believe in myself in my very lowest times. All your Leela pictures and videos during my writing marathon pulled me over the finish line!

> **Liv:** Pana, I will never forget when we first met: You knew exactly the right things to say so I wouldn't be scared while everything was so busy around Charlotte. It's very special how much our hearts have connected over the years since. I know you, Conrad, and Leela will be part of so many chapters in my life story. I am so lucky to have PanaLove. Thank you forever.

Cynthia: Thank you to Heather Lang for being a reader, thinker, and supporter of this book even in its proposal form. Liv and I are so grateful to have your keen eye for detail, but also your incredible heart for supporting our craziness around sharing this story. Thanks for the rudder you provided both of us, and on a more practical level, the space (my writing nest) you provided me in your home to write uninterrupted, and for all the times you brought me tea just when I needed it (who knew I was a tea drinker?). Without that, this book would have never been finished. Liv will probably say she loves you most, but I sure am a close second.

Liv: Heather, I have so much love for you in my heart, it makes me wish for you over and over again. Thank you for all the times you answered my texts even when you were tired or busy. You know how to understand kids, and most especially me. You've taught me how to be more patient in my work, and how to understand words more deeply. You're my forever person, and when there are more LivBit adventures, I know you will be right there cheering me on. Saying I love you doesn't seem like enough, so instead I'll say, I wish for more of you, and I hope knowing that gives you heartbeeps.

Cynthia: Thank you to Valerie Witte for her unending support of our work, and her continued enthusiasm for the many dimensions of connectedness Liv and I continue to work on together. We are also grateful to the ISTE team for taking a chance on having a mum and kid writing team work together for publication. We feel honored to be the first, but we also know we won't be the last.

Liv: Valerie, you were the first big boss who knew our story mattered enough to be a book. And you helped us find the perfect Dutch orange for our cover and made sure it had some heartbeeps too. I'm so grateful we are book buddies forever now, and I hope our work makes you so proud.

Cynthia: I want to acknowledge my incredible co-writer, thinker, biggest heartbeeper, Liv for all the incredible ways she shares her thinking with so many people, and most especially what she shares with me. I'm so grateful the universe picked me to be your muma.

Liv: Muma, it's so special the way you believe in kids. I hope when you see this book on people's bookshelves you will know your words matter so much to so many people. But mostly, I hope you know that more than your words, your heart matters most. I love you!

Cynthia: Finally, thanks to our family, and especially Matt, husband and daddy, who puts aside many things to support the work Liv and I do together, and also thank you to Charlotte and Quinn, who tolerate a lot of tech and book talk in our house. We are so proud to share this journey with the world, but we are most proud to share it with those closest to us. You are the truest and biggest heartbeeps behind this work.

Liv: Heartbeeps to my family! Daddy, you always give me the best jokes for my presentations! You know exactly how to make people laugh hard. Quinn, you are the best believing brother ever! And, Charlotte, I just know you are going to give the world more stories, and I am so happy I get to help you! I love all of you sooooo much!

Introduction

Even the smallest person can change the course of the future.

—J. R. R. TOLKIEN

Spark Change introduces you to Liv, a young changemaker, empowered to use digital tools to create content and share online. Liv's story offers us an opportunity to share how she's using technology as a tool for empathy, equity, and activism. In Liv's work, she often uses the word *heartbeep* to explain a moment when she feels deeply about a cause, her learning, and the understanding she gains. This book will offer many heartbeep ideas for work with your students.

Since she introduced me already, let me introduce the other voice in this text: my mum, Cynthia. She's a true believer in student voice and has one of the biggest hearts for finding ways to help all kids share their stories with the world. My mum helps me, but she's also a helper to so many others. She loves kids, books, and tech in that order. She didn't have very many people helping her when she was a kid, so as a grown-up she's become a magnet to kids with lots of needs. Books and tech tools have always been a way she's created relationships and understanding in her work. Her consulting work takes her to lots and lots of interesting places all over the world, and I feel so lucky I get to join forces with her to write this book!

What my mum didn't say in her fancy introduction of me, is that I'm the creator of LivBits. LivBits are short videos I make for kids and teachers; they share a little bit of me, Liv, and a little bit of my thinking, Bits. Put that all together, and you have LivBits! This has been my passion project since I was eight years old. I started LivBits based on work my mum was doing as a faculty member at the University of New Hampshire. Each week, she'd have her graduate students make short videos where they would reflect by talking about their teaching internships. Many of her graduate students started using this activity with their own students. These elementary students talked about their thinking as readers, and I just loved watching their videos over and over again. I was fascinated by how kids talked about books they loved, and I thought to myself, I can make those kinds of videos too!

And the absolute truth is, I had no idea Liv's videos would become so popular—and neither of us could have imagined back then that we'd be writing a book together about this journey. I encouraged Liv to create and share her thinking this way to help her make sense of bullying she experienced in second grade. I wanted Liv to have a project where she could see herself the way I saw her: caring, smart, and resourceful. I knew if she talked about her reading, she'd get feedback from people other than me, and maybe she'd believe in herself a little more.

Yes! And what happened after I made those first few videos empowered me very, very much! I realized I had a voice that mattered to the world. I realized I could create something that was uniquely mine. And I saw how much the world appreciated it.

Maybe you've watched one of my LivBit videos, heard me speak at a conference, engaged with me in a Twitter chat, read one of my blog posts, or even met me in person. If you have, you've seen my videos aren't fancy, they are just quick selfie videos. This is important because we want people who read this book to know it's not about the flashiness of the tech, but about the depth of the thinking that can happen when kids share their passions.

I have a super favorite book by Paul Fleischman called *Joyful Noise: Poems for Two Voices* (1988). The book is meant to be read with alternating voices, and it's so fun to hear how special the poems become when you combine the voices together. When I was little, I'd often pick this book to be read to me before bed, and because I had many of the poems memorized, I could be the second voice in the poem.

> Although you can read the book with just a solo voice, the experience is so much richer when you read it with the other voice in mind!
>
> So, my mum, Cynthia, and I offer you the chance to read this professional text as if it were a poem for two voices. As you think about the ideas we share here, I hope you always hold onto my voice, a kid who is making her mark on the world by using tech tools. When you read my words, think back to your own students, and consider how powerful the story becomes when their voices can be added to mine.

And my voice in this book is distinct in an important way, as well. First, I offer my teacher perspective, but of course, I am first and foremost mum to Liv. The challenge of writing this text together is about voice(s) and consideration for how you, the reader, will reason through the importance of each. I invite you to consider the power of our voices together and experience how multiple narratives add powerful insight into student creation. (Note: Throughout the book, most of Liv's text will be indicated with a vertical line on the left side and in a different font from my text, so you can immediately know which of us is speaking.)

Recently, Liv brought me a page from our family word-a-day calendar. We have a daily tradition of sharing a word and deciding if we've ever heard it, read it, or used it in everyday conversation. We alternate days with the goal to stump one another with the word. Her word definitely stumped me: *tūrangawaewae* [tə,rʌŋgə'weɪweɪ]. In fact, I couldn't even pronounce it without saying it very, very slowly first. I still have to see it to say it—*tūrangawaewae*. But the meaning is one I'll never forget—a place to stand:

> "Tūrangawaewae is one of the most well-known and powerful Māori concepts. Literally tūranga (standing place), waewae (feet), it is often translated as 'a place to stand.' Tūrangawaewae are places where we feel especially empowered and connected. They are our foundation, our place in the world, our home." (Royal, 2007)

Liv and I laughed at how the calendar seemed to bless us with a giant idea just as we were in the midst of writing this book.

And because we LOVE words so much, we'll be offering you many in this text. Our hope is that these words act as powerful sparks igniting the conversations we hope you'll have in your communities, especially around the ideas of student voice, citizenship, and creating with the world in mind.

You've already heard my own special word, heartbeep, and now we offer *tūrangawaewae* as another spark to light the way through this text. I hope you say this word out loud right now. Do it. Say the word *tūrangawaewae*. Say it more than once until it rolls off your tongue, like you're in everyday conversation. Ask someone you love, "What's your *tūrangawaewae*—your place to stand?"

In today's connected world, it's no longer a question of whether students are going to be using a device; it's about supporting students to create, reason, and connect responsibly. But how do we help students find a place to stand—their *tūrangawaewae*?

What This Book Is and Isn't

Spark Change isn't a book intended to provide a digital citizenship curriculum. A number of books already focus on defining students' online interactions, so instead, this book focuses on the purpose of being a connected learner. None of us can ignore the fact that the line between personal and digital interaction is disappearing quickly as technology becomes more a part of our everyday world. Our focus, therefore, should be on teaching students how to behave in *all* the spaces they interact. When we teach students to behave the same way online as they do in person, the focus is less about the appropriateness of digital space and more about becoming good humans. To do that, why not take advantage of all the opportunities available to them?

Because this book is about how to interact with those around us and not about specific social media platforms, it should remain relevant no matter what new social media platforms arise.

Liv's Digital Citizenship Definition

- Be a good person.
- Be a critical thinker.
- Be an advocate for something you care about.

As Liv often shares in her keynote speeches, citizenship is centered on three simple ideals: be a good person, be a critical thinker, and be an advocate for something you care about in life.

> When I first started my LivBit work and I wanted to post about it, I'd brainstorm with my mum what the post could include. She'd encourage me to synthesize the big idea and share it with a hashtag—words that would help my audience feel enthusiastic about my work. I discovered that I was very good at hashtagging something I am sort of known for, and you'll see many of them shared throughout this book. Hashtags are a really powerful way to frame your own thinking, but in online platforms, they also work to directly connect you to others using the same tag. In many ways, kids can understand their work more when they see it synthesized in this way; it's like zooming in on the big idea.

Much of the dialogue around children and connectedness centers on fear and safety related to age and privacy. Although this book will discuss several key techniques Liv uses to stay safe online, it's not meant as a referendum on safety, nor is it any sort of dissertation on the argument of age restrictions and privacy. In our view, very little we do anymore is truly private. We are continually surveilled and monitored in our everyday lives whether we see proof of it or not. Liv's work online represents such a massive piece of her identity as a learner, it would be cruel to limit her access because of age restrictions. We lead the book with an examination of rights and restrictions, and we hope to provide you with insight for conversations in your communities.

Liv's Hashtags for the World

- #LivBits
- #KeepReading
- #KeepThinking
- #KidsCanTeachUs
- #Heartbeeps
- #SparkChange

And I have something to say about age and restrictions. I know lots of kids who make better decisions online than some grown-ups. In my three years creating and sharing, I've seen so many examples of poor behavior by adults. In fact, many prominent leaders are not leaders for me online. The story they create isn't one that inspires me to want to love the world, it's one that often makes me more fearful. So, age to me doesn't imply maturity and good decision-making. An age restriction is a number adults come up with as a rule. In my opinion, parents and teachers should guide kids at a younger age, when they listen more carefully, so citizenship skills become more automatic from what they create and experience.

This book will examine the power of partnerships with schools, teachers, communities, and families in digital learning. Each chapter leads with a question and a written "Bit" by Liv. Then I extend the chapter by providing practical examples and grounding the work in theory. Although the larger topics of *Spark Change* are digital connectedness and digital citizenship, the book will also highlight Liv as a digital leader and the power of authentic student voice and participation.

Our work is positioned with a digital mindset, but it reaches into Liv's literate life. Everything Liv creates is an example of her literacy understanding, and part of the book's message is the consideration that in a digital world, children need connected literacy experiences.

Liv's Twitter feed is flooded with teachers sharing how she influences students; in each chapter, we will include these stories from the field extending the work Liv does, as well as examples from my consulting work.

When children create online, they learn directly about their own voice and citizenship. With this in mind, each chapter will feature examples of Liv's work as well as Spotlight profiles of other children making an impact on the digital world through creation and participation. We hope these Spotlights, which are written by Liv based on interviews with the subjects, invite deeper connection to the ideas presented in every chapter and provide an entry point into using tech in more robust and innovative ways with your own students. We hope you will share these Spotlights in your own classrooms to ignite and inspire children to follow their passions using tech.

> Kids are naturally curious about the world around them! We want ways to learn more, care more, and love more, and using digital tools allows us to do this. We can't have you read any more of this book without this incredible reminder from a second-grade friend in Connecticut:

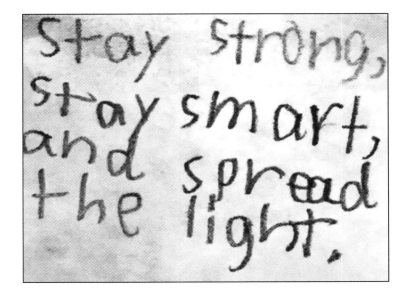

That's what we hope *Spark Change* brings to you as a reader—the ability to stay strong, stay smart, and spread light—your first *tūrangawaewae* consideration. Let's create sparks together!

Connection to ISTE Standards

The ISTE Standards provide a powerful and meaningful rudder for the work Liv presents in this book. All of her LivBit work can be adapted to the classroom and function as student activities. Aside from the LivBit examples, we have included a "Lesson Ideas to Try" section featuring activities from other teachers in the field who have explored our ideas even more deeply.

Each chapter leads with an invitation to you as a reader and highlights the ISTE Standards for Educators (iste.org/standards/for-educators) that align with the chapter topic. We hope this helps you extend your thinking into theory, practice, and student creation and understanding. The following chart outlines the Educator Standards covered in each chapter.

	1 Learner	2 Leader	3 Citizen	4 Collaborator	5 Designer	6 Facilitator	7 Analyst
Chapter 1		2a, 2b, 2c				6a, 6b, 6c, 6d	
Chapter 2	1a, 1b, 1c, 1d				5a, 5b, 5c, 5d		
Chapter 3		2a, 2b, 2c, 2d	3a, 3b, 3c, 3d			6a, 6b, 6c, 6d	
Chapter 4				4a, 4b, 4c, 4d			
Chapter 5			3a, 3b, 3c, 3d			6a, 6b, 6c, 6d	
Chapter 6	1a, 1b, 1c						7a, 7b, 7c
Chapter 7		2a, 2b, 2c, 2d				6a, 6b, 6c, 6d	

Our student Spotlights also align with the ISTE Standards for Students (iste.org/standards/for-students), and the following chart shows how Liv's stories, activities, and examples support the Student Standards.

	1 Empowered Student	2 Digital Citizen	3 Knowledge Constructor	4 Innovative Designer	5 Computational Thinker	6 Creative Communicator	7 Global Collaborator
Chapter 1		2a, 2b, 2c, 2d	3d			6a, 6d	7b
Chapter 2	1a, 1b, 1c, 1d	2a, 2b, 2c, 2d					7b, 7d
Chapter 3	1a, 1b, 1c, 1d	2a, 2b, 2c, 2d	3a, 3b, 3d	4a, 4b, 4c, 4d	5b	6a, 6b, 6c, 6d	7b, 7d
Chapter 4	1a, 1b, 1c, 1d	2a, 2b, 2d	3a, 3b, 3c, 3d	4a, 4b, 4d		6a, 6b, 6c, 6d	7a, 7b, 7c, 7d
Chapter 5	1a, 1b, 1c, 1d	2a, 2b	3a, 3b, 3c, 3d			6a, 6b, 6c, 6d	7a, 7b, 7c, 7d
Chapter 6	1a, 1b, 1c, 1d		3a, 3c, 3d	4a, 4b, 4c, 4d		6a, 6b, 6c, 6d	7a, 7b, 7c, 7d
Chapter 7	1a, 1b, 1c, 1d	2a, 2b, 2c, 2d					7a, 7b, 7c, 7d
Spotlights	Jordyn Zimmerman	#ICANHELP	Nate Butkus, Sadie Bugnitz	Louie DaCosta		Norah Meekins	Sara Abou Rashed

Chapter One

Digital Rights

> Have you ever considered whether connected learning is a digital right?

Recently, my mum told me a story about a second grader who was in the audience when I was hosting a book conversation with an author in New York City. The audience included over 1,000 students, and the energy in the auditorium was filled with heartbeeps.

The author writes incredible nonfiction books about amazing creatures, and the little boy was sitting behind my mum bouncing happily in his seat as the author talked about her books. A few times, my mum glanced to admire the little boy because his happiness was so strong she could feel it all around her. He also clutched an iPad and was pointing at it over and over again trying to get my mum's attention.

My mum realized the little boy struggled with speech, and pointing at his iPad was his way of trying to get a message across. She turned and told the boy she knew me and the author, and she asked if he wanted her to take a picture of his iPad so we'd get his message.

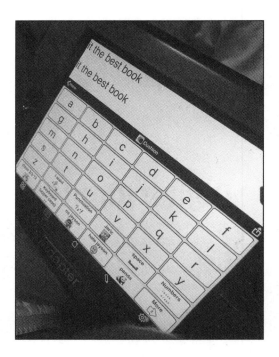

He was so overjoyed, he jumped to his feet and flung his iPad into my mum's lap!

The boy had written the sweetest message to the author ("It the best book"), and he felt determined to get it to me so I could let her know. Using his iPad, this student was able to convey a simple but powerful opinion, and my mum taking the picture and promising to share it with us showed this boy his message was important.

I share this story at the beginning of our book as a way to emphasize what my mum and I mean when we say access to technology is a digital right. This boy, for example, has a right to communicate with the world. In his hands, technology is a powerful and necessary means for him to learn and grow. Taking away his iPad would be super mean because that would limit his ability to communicate effectively. This student's voice matters as much as the voices of students who shouted their messages to the author from the audience. The only difference is that he needed his device to shout his message for him.

I like to call myself a book activist. I like to share the power of books in kids' lives. But I'm also an activist for kids and technology. Grown-ups would never think to snatch away a book to punish a kid, but they don't think twice about taking away tech.

Kids aren't waiting to have digital access. Some of us are demanding it from grown-ups. That's how the Parkland, Florida, kids harnessed a movement. They didn't wait for the grown-ups to give them permission; they showed the grown-ups how they could use their digital access to create a movement many grown-ups could never have predicted.

But guess what? Kids could predict it. Kids understand technology has the power to create change. We understand how important having digital access is for our learning. Kids understand we can change the world by our creations—whether it's a simple message on an iPad to an author or a massive movement to demand change around gun laws.

Kids get it. We know access to technology is a right we all deserve, and, if necessary, we'll find a workaround to get it.

Technology isn't a privilege only some kids deserve. It's a right we should protect for all kids. Kids in other parts of the world often do not have access like kids here in the United States. In many ways, we are so fortunate to have access, but this also means we have a greater responsibility to help other kids gain access too. LivBits has made me more aware of the world and of my own privilege. It's helped me develop empathy for kids who are less fortunate.

Recently, my mum returned from a work trip in the very northern part of our home state New Hampshire, almost at the Canadian border. The school she was consulting at is tiny—only 26 students from kindergarten through sixth grade. Many kids in that community have access to technology only when they are at school. More than half of the students don't have Wi-Fi at home. Sometimes it's because their homes are hidden deeply in the woods, so service is spotty and unreliable. And sometimes it's because they don't even have running water, so there's no way they could have Wi-Fi.

So, when my mum came home a little sad from her trip, I was worried that maybe our work wasn't powerful enough. Maybe our story didn't matter very much to the world. But instead my mum shared with me how much her brain was lingering in that mountain school.

I've learned a lot of big words and ideas doing my LivBit work, and especially writing this book. In this case, I learned how to think more deeply about *equity*. Equity means considering fairness from lots of angles and lots of perspectives. My mum shared how guilty she felt not thinking about equity more deliberately in her everyday work in this particular little school. She shared how lots of times, lack of equity with technology is so easy for her to see in urban areas. But when she was in the mountains, she realized she had to look and think a bit differently about this idea. In cities, schools can do creative things like park a Wi-Fi bus in a public space and invite families to take advantage. But in rural areas, this can't really work because many families may not even have transportation or would have to travel many miles to access a Wi-Fi bus because they live too far apart to gather easily.

My mum's worries showed me even more deeply how important it is for grown-ups to consider technology as a digital right. Having access to technology tools at school is sometimes the only way some kids can digitally create and explore. In these circumstances, it's even more important that access isn't taken away because of misbehavior. If it is taken away, then kids have no way to experience creating with technology or being connected to a world outside of their immediate environment.

LivBits started as a home project, but now I see it as a world project. I want more kids to have the opportunity to be creators and to share their reading and thinking in bigger ways. If you are too scared to use technology or to have kids on social media, I hope this book shifts your mindset. I hope you'll see the value of technology, creating with

Connection to the ISTE Standards

Educator Standard 2: Leader

Educators seek out opportunities for leadership to support student empowerment and success and to improve teaching and learning. Educators:

a. Shape, advance and accelerate a shared vision for empowered learning with technology by engaging with education stakeholders.

b. Advocate for equitable access to educational technology, digital content and learning opportunities to meet the diverse needs of all students.

c. Model for colleagues the identification, exploration, evaluation, curation and adoption of new digital resources and tools for learning.

Educator Standard 6: Facilitator

Educators facilitate learning with technology to support student achievement of the ISTE Standards for Students. Educators:

a. Foster a culture where students take ownership of their learning goals and outcomes in both independent and group settings.

b. Manage the use of technology and student learning strategies in digital platforms, virtual environments, hands-on makerspaces or in the field.

c. Create learning opportunities that challenge students to use a design process and computational thinking to innovate and solve problems.

d. Model and nurture creativity and creative expression to communicate ideas, knowledge or connections.

the world in mind, and having access to platforms for feedback. The positives these platforms offer far outweigh any negatives, and any negatives can be used as teaching and learning moments.

I leave you with a few call-to-action questions:

- Will you be the kind of grown-up who will stand strong for kids and tech?

- Will you help those who have less access to get more?

- Will you pledge not to take away a device for misbehavior, and instead, use the moment to teach the student?

- Will you be the kind of grown-up who sparks change around kids and tech?

Understanding Digital Access as a Right for Kids

Liv's rich experiences online are possible for several reasons. First, she's been empowered to view herself as a creator—she understands the power of sharing her story with the world. Next, her digital crew looks out for her safety, and Liv accesses them when needed. Finally, Liv has developed the confidence to navigate online platforms, and she seeks out ways to understand questionable or challenging feedback.

It's important to question equity and access when considering Liv's experiences online. She's had access since an early age, along with explicit guidance to broaden her understanding of tricky situations. Liv has mentioned how powerful she feels her voice is for the world, and it's true; I see this as a right she deserves. Her online work is another literacy pathway and just as important as her right to books and schooling.

During a recent school visit, a teacher pulled Liv aside and somewhat apologetically shared with her that she "didn't believe in using devices with her students." This teacher went on to share that although she loved Liv's work, she wouldn't be encouraging her students to watch any of Liv's videos, because "kids waste too much time online already."

It's interesting this teacher viewed Liv's work highly but couldn't seem to understand the importance of this type of creation for her own students. Her judgment of how devices are used and the time spent on them clouded her ability to view student creation as an essential piece of their literate lives. Restricting access to students because of misconceptions or personal judgments isn't acceptable. A teacher's attitude toward tech can make or break student access—keeping them from the very tool that might help them understand themselves more deeply as thinkers.

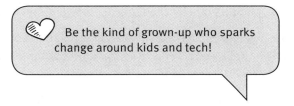

Be the kind of grown-up who sparks change around kids and tech!

If teachers share an unwillingness to support children and tech, Liv is confident enough to question their perception by asking a simple question: "Would you take books away from your students?"

Most of the time, she knows the teacher's answer—no. Children need access to tech tools to learn just as they need books to learn. Books provide opportunities for children to consider perspectives and create meaning that can influence who they become. Tech tools do this as well.

Viewing digital access as a right for children is important and not a new consideration for those working in the area of global digital access. In a recent interview, Patrick Geary, UNICEF's children's rights expert, shared how parents are one piece of the puzzle when considering children's rights online and elsewhere. He suggested it takes a concerted effort from teachers and the community at large to protect, respect, and realize children's rights (Poynton, 2018). UNICEF's research in the area of worldwide digital access for children has resulted in their strong position that children's rights include digital access. Online platforms have vastly changed how children learn and express themselves, and as UNICEF's research details, it's not acceptable to limit

> Have your students write a list of digital rights for your class! Use a device to record your class list of digital rights, and post it in a place where your students can get feedback. Add a hashtag to each right so your audience will see the power of your class vision for using technology tools.

access based on assumptions adults may hold, especially when adults haven't grown up in this rapidly changing digital age (Poynton, 2018).

Jasmina Byrne, who leads UNICEF's research on children and internet access, as well as family and parenting support, points out in *Children's Rights and the Internet: From Guidelines to Practice*:

> "It is important to remember that child rights are universal and equally applicable everywhere in the world, irrespective of the age or gender of the child, whether they go to school or not, are rich or poor. And that should be the same when it comes to the internet. Why should we think that rights, when applied to the internet, are any different? What we could do as parents or educators . . . is really to make sure that we build [children's] skills, capacities and their resilience, but also to improve our own relationships and communications with them—and trust—so that children will come and tell us when things happen."

Youth safety and citizenship expert Anne Collier agrees and questions the arbitrary age of 13 as a starting point for student experience on social media platforms. Collier argues for consideration of student readiness around civic engagement, reminding us most children are ready for this kind of participation well before thirteen. She notes the passions young children demonstrate and the desires they have to contribute to their communities focused on those passions (2018). I can attest to this with Liv's love of books, my youngest daughter's passion for nature (and her annoyance any time we don't remember our reusable grocery bags), and my son's non-stop expert talk about building entire communities with LEGOs.

Truthfully, the real question isn't about the "perfect" age for access to devices; it's about whether the child is developmentally ready to have access to an online world. This book gives explicit examples of the groundwork needed to prepare children for healthy and responsible device use. Having access at school to devices can help with student readiness, but having wider community and parental support is essential.

In my literacy work with teachers, I talk a lot about how to encourage and motivate students in their reading lives. This includes exploring new genres and themes with students and explicitly considering the complexity students will encounter in these new experiences, then designing teaching around these considerations. This is no different from helping students navigate the complexity they experience online. If we imagine social media platforms as a type of narrative, it becomes clearer how crucial it is to give children the tools to create meaning there.

Supporting and Encouraging Responsible Tech Use

Introducing responsible device use is an important consideration for teachers—like modeling book choice for independent reading or encouraging students to eat healthy snacks. Rather than having a fixed mindset around technology use and screen time, consider the opportunities device usage in the classroom provides for helping students demonstrate proper etiquette and test out rules for online participation. More and more school communities have one-to-one initiatives or at least give students some level of access to devices for learning, so it's imperative we move beyond device usage for testing purposes and foster a creation-based attitude with students. Of course, safety is always a consideration, and this book offers what's possible when adults participate in co-creation and guide student presence online.

You would never hand a kindergartener a chapter book and expect them to figure out how to decode all the words or understand the meaning on their own; you'd explicitly support and unpack the book at a word and meaning level. The same scaffolding approach holds true for students' tech experiences. Like books, devices have nuanced complexity that requires users to make decisions and consider choices that either enhance the experience or create confusion. App choice and platform participation requires students to understand how to ask themselves questions as they go, just as they would reading a book: What's happening here? How does this help me as a learner? Who can help me understand this better?

The question of when to get a child their own phone has been superseded by the challenge of finding the right balance of device usage. By the time parents consider making this milestone purchase, many students may have already had many experiences making digital decisions and being responsible with school-issued devices. This leads to many important questions: How can parents make sure children stay protected—while also remaining empowered? How do we encourage a partnership between home and school that develops a healthy mindset for student participation and creation online? Knowing digital experiences are essential in a global society, how can we advocate more vigorously for students who lack online access? Further, how can we demand a shift from fearmongering to providing examples of students participating and creating safely with the world in mind?

Any interaction with children to help them navigate the world— digital and non-digital—is beneficial for their development. This book isn't advocating for digital co-creation or co-viewing at the expense of non-digital interactions. Rather, Liv's experiences have been successful because she shares what she learns from her mentors and becomes a guide and facilitator for others. #KidsCanTeachUs is her biggest message. Initially, Liv needed conversations about how digital tools and media functioned so she could create and manage her LivBit work in a responsible manner. All of Liv's experiences with tech tools have enhanced Liv's non-tech learning. They complement each other and are so interwoven that it's impossible to see one as more important than the other. For example, interacting with authors and teachers online inspires Liv to read and research more, which invites more creation of LivBit videos, blogs, and Liv's Lists. This never-ending creation loop empowers her as a learner.

Liv was recently working with kindergarten students, and I heard her prompting them on how to reasonably consider the power of sharing with AirDrop. (AirDrop is an easy and quick way to share content between Apple devices via Wi-Fi and Bluetooth.) Liv directed the group of students by saying, "I'm only expecting a video from Daphne, so does that mean any of you will try to AirDrop to me? Nooooooo, because we're responsible digital citizens! And we know AirDropping should be something your friend expects!" Hearing her remind the group in this way made me more aware of a simple share technique and the etiquette behind it. I'd never considered connecting this to a digital citizenship behavior, but as soon as I heard her say this, it made perfect sense.

Initially, the conversations Liv and I had about her LivBit work empowered and informed how I guided her navigation of digital tools and the platforms where she was sharing. Now, I learn more from letting Liv lead and hearing how she reasons and manages her work on and offline, as well as how she shares this knowledge with others. Her wisdom-filled thinking often stuns me, and I feel humbled by her insights.

Vygotsky's (1978) constructivist view of learning asserts that all learning is social. When we factor in the use of technology, the social opportunities become richer and more dynamic for students. Learning experiences are now interwoven with technology, and the tools children use help them understand themselves as learners. Still, many people see technology as a privilege we allow children to have, rather than a right they deserve. I'm not sure how much further we need to go into the future for this mindset to shift, but Liv and I hope your engagement with this book is an indication of your commitment to help inform others.

Let this be the first step in many to follow. Demand digital access as a right all children deserve.

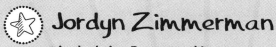

Jordyn Zimmerman

@jordynbzim: Empowered Learner

I heard Jordyn's story at my friend Alan November's Building Learning Communities conference in Boston, Massachusetts. Jordyn has autism and uses an iPad to speak. She was Alan's kid keynote speaker the summer before I was his keynote speaker. I knew Jordyn's words had moved the crowd so much, she'd received a standing ovation. Since then, I've followed Jordyn's work, and I can honestly say there isn't another person who inspires me more.

Jordyn's story is compelling. Her experiences should make everyone think about student rights, expectations, and access to technology for learning. The way Jordyn thinks about rights gives me so many heartbeeps. She said, "When I think of the word *rights*, I imagine all students having access to technology, in order to extend their reach and abilities. When technology is intentionally used, it benefits all users—and for many children, this can change the trajectory of their lives."

Imagine not having any way to talk with others. That's the challenge Jordyn faced for eighteen years. As she explained, "My words were trapped inside of my uncontrollable body. Unable to converse with others, I could not share my intact thoughts with the world. When I began to use an iPad, first by exhaustively touching pictures and then by touching letters to make words, I was able to show my intellect."

Jordyn is so grateful that technology has given her a voice so she could share her ideas and have relationships with others. But she worries about all the other people who are stuck in silence. If you met Jordyn, you would immediately sense her passion to help others find their voices. She hopes people will learn to never make assumptions about other people's competence, because, as she said, "when people make assumptions, they miss out on others' strengths, words, and stories."

Jordyn is a trailblazer for students with disabilities. Through her persistence and her advocacy for others, she's giving the world an incredible amount of heartbeeps. I am inspired by her words, deeds, and her vision for kids. Here's how she described her proudest accomplishment:

> "As a nonspeaking student, I was never on track to attend college. However, at the age of 21, I graduated from high school with acceptances to the four universities to which I had applied—a [substantial] accomplishment. While I am the first nonspeaking autistic student at Ohio University, I hope my work is blazing the trail for future students who type to communicate."

Jordyn's hashtag for the world: #TeachTheWorld

Chapter Two

Digital Purpose

> Have you ever thought about how you connect your students to what MATTERS in the world?

Not long ago, I did a school visit in a small town in western Massachusetts. Three school communities packed an elementary school auditorium, creating an exciting and electric buzz around my LivBit work. Teachers shared my LivBit videos before the visit, so it felt as if many kids needed a few confirmations from me. First, they needed to see I was a "real" kid, not just a digital mirage. Next, they wanted to know if I sounded just like I sound in my videos—basically, do I talk fast and as if I just saw a unicorn out in the parking lot? Yes! I do! All of those wonders were easily confirmed. Finally, and maybe the hardest confirmation, they wanted to ask loads of one-of-a-kind kid questions—the kind I can never feel fully prepared to answer. Luckily, the one-of-a-kind questions at this visit were ones that created instant heartbeeps for me and the crowd. In other words, I didn't leave the visit rethinking any of my answers. In fact, I felt proudest of my final one—so much so, that's it's become a central message in all of my subsequent school visits.

An adorable and wisdom-filled third grader stood up and asked excitedly, "Liv, how does it feel to be famous?" I didn't even hesitate in my response. My LivBit work has never been about becoming famous; it's always been about finding interesting ways to share my story with the world, to continuously create and share more and more. I answered with what has become a LivBit mantra: "I'm not famous, I'm global!"

My answer was followed by raucous cheers from the kid-filled audience.

Later, my mum and I discussed the students' joyful reactions to my answer. In the moment, their cheers felt like a massive hug around my body. Even as I write this now, I get such a huge heartbeep remembering that visit. I'm so grateful to those kids for encouraging and believing in the purpose of my LivBit work. But their cheers also showed us two very important things: Kids want to have purpose in their connected lives, and they can think beyond being famous when they are given examples of other kids creating an online story. If we begin the citizenship work with an emphasis around

Connection to the ISTE Standards

Educator Standard 1: Learner

Educators continually improve their practice by learning from and with others and exploring proven and promising practices that leverage technology to improve student learning. Educators:

a. Set professional learning goals to explore and apply pedagogical approaches made possible by technology and reflect on their effectiveness.

b. Pursue professional interests by creating and actively participating in local and global learning networks.

c. Stay current with research that supports improved student learning outcomes, including findings from the learning sciences.

Educator Standard 5: Designer

Educators design authentic, learner-driven activities and environments that recognize and accommodate learner variability. Educators:

a. Use technology to create, adapt and personalize learning experiences that foster independent learning and accommodate learner differences and needs.

b. Design authentic learning activities that align with content area standards and use digital tools and resources to maximize active, deep learning.

c. Explore and apply instructional design principles to create innovative digital learning environments that engage and support learning.

---

creation, kids will develop a mindset that includes purpose. Since so often the conversation about connectedness centers on safety, kids develop a mindset of fear, and maybe that fear develops into secretiveness as they grow older. Kids are going to make mistakes in life. Connectedness might mean those mistakes are magnified to a much wider audience, but that also means there is an opportunity for more feedback and support. Focusing on the fear only creates division between kids and adults. As you read this chapter, I hope you think about what really matters to kids online, and how we can create movements in these spaces that are bigger than anyone ever imagined.

Feeling the Pulse of Digital Connection

When Liv was just a toddler, she'd walk around with her hand on her heart. Most people assumed she was taking some sweet patriotic stance, but when questioned, she'd grab your hand and place it on her heart, asking, "Do you feel my heart beep?" This became an immediate and favorite "Liv-ism" in our family—a tender way she described many of her experiences. She seemed to always be exclaiming, "heartbeeps!" It's as if navigating the world was so joyful, Liv immediately felt a small "beep" in her heart, and she wanted to share that beep with everyone.

> Sharing your passions with the world creates heartbeeps! Do more of what you love; the world will notice from the heartbeep trail that follows you!

Fast forward to some of Liv's first interactions online, where she began to take on the space with the same *joie de vivre* she had as a toddler. Her heartbeep stance helped her feel more freely the pulse of digital connections. She saw every interaction as an opportunity to truly feel something—to experience the world's heartbeeps. Her earliest posts were more often than not hashtagged with this special brand of joy, and it was evident her followers felt joy as they interacted with her. From the very beginning, Liv navigated these spaces as if her followers' hands were right on her heart; together, they created many heartbeep stories.

Isn't this a powerful way of imagining the digital spaces we frequent? Imagine your posts having the potential to create intense emotion, so intense a follower can feel it in her heart. Now imagine this emotion turning into an action, a movement, or a powerful story that can change the world. People reading your posts see themselves as part of your story, and it motivates them to share your story more widely. Maybe it motivates them to share their own story too; it releases an inner drive for them to be a part of something bigger. This drive gives them a direction, a purpose.

Contextualizing the Work

In his book *Drive: The Surprising Truth About What Motivates Us*, Daniel Pink (2009) asserts that the secret to high performance and satisfaction is the deeply human need to direct our lives, to learn and create new things, and to make the world a better place. Heavily influenced by Deci & Ryan's (1985) theory of self-determination, Pink's work challenges early, deeply entrenched notions on biological and extrinsic motivation. It offers a more robust and nuanced definition by examining intrinsic factors influencing our decision-making processes. Pink offers three specific elements on motivation we can use as lenses to view student online work: autonomy, mastery, and purpose. Contextualizing Liv's work with these lenses offers an example of how students develop a sense of purpose and, ultimately, agency as learners.

Autonomy

Liv's work has created an explosion of opportunities that continues to grow her identity as a learner. Initially, she made videos to share her messages, but now she's a blogger, podcaster, and speaker, as well. All of this came from one short 60-second video she created at the age of 8. Liv sees herself as a creator of content, and as she works to grow her content, she adds dimensions to herself as a learner, inspiring a

Creation Loop

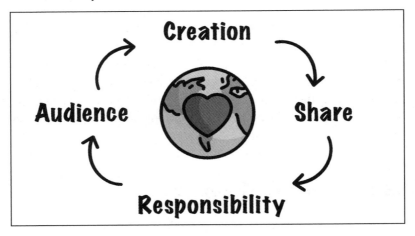

sense of autonomy and confidence people immediately notice when they engage with her.

Liv makes decisions guided by a strong sense of purpose, and she is empowered by the myriad of decisions she makes to magnify her LivBit work. If you analyze her interactions online, you immediately sense the care Liv brings to her relationships, what Noddings (1984) described as an ethic of care.

Imagine if all children were charged with this ethic in their citizenship work. Noddings defines care by rooting it in receptivity, relatedness, and responsiveness (p. 2). The elements of care Noddings suggests give us a way to nudge Pink's motivational research further, by describing the feeling someone might experience from connectedness. It's essential we encourage a deep sense of commitment to reciprocity in our connected work. In other words, we develop a creation loop for students: We create to share, with sharing comes a responsibility, and with responsibility comes consideration for our audience. Ideally, the feedback received in this creation loop provides enough to keep a continuous process for creation.

If students care more about the people they are impacting with their work, they can better understand the purpose and power of their message. This gives them motivation to be confident creators of new content and begin the cycle all over again. When this happens, students gain a deeper sense of autonomy.

Mastery

An interesting concept to consider as a creator is the idea of mastery. Liv sees the potential of everything she creates as an opportunity for feedback from a global audience. The mastery lens is widened by a continuous feedback loop that happens when we involve tech tools in student creation. Consider the simple selfie as an example. Most people have a selfie stance: They cock their head toward the best light, lift their chin, make sure their eyes don't look wonky, and give whatever expression the moment demands as they snap the picture. In all of this, the selfie taker is tacitly considering their audience. The secret of selfie mastery comes in the feedback the image garners after it's shared with an audience. In other words, the learner can ask: What can I do better next time to gesture toward mastery?

It's important to consider mastery doesn't imply being at the end of the creation cycle. Mastery means finding more ways to improve your later creations. In short, studying more ways to capture the best selfie means mastering an understanding of what your audience demands.

Purpose

The largest construct of this chapter rests on the shoulders of a succinct definition of purpose in digital spaces. But first consider this: Pink's success as a researcher comes from his playfulness with theory, as well as his ability to tell a fantastic story. He helps us see his unique take on the world and get a clearer definition of purpose. Zooming in on purpose, we can define it as seeing a range of possibilities to learn more, illuminating a student's worldview, and sparking her sense of agency. When all these pieces fall into place, a student feels empowered and develops a solid sense of her identity as a learner—with purpose comes power.

Purpose of LivBits

After many collaborative presenting opportunities, Liv created a slide representing the purpose of her LivBit videos. Her words came from ideas she heard me say again and again when people asked, "What's the purpose of this kind of work?" It always surprised Liv how often we'd get asked this question, because the purpose was so clear to her: She saw her thinking as important. Creating videos gave Liv incredible opportunities to linger in a reflective stance and consider the big ideas of a book. She could also gather insightful feedback from her audience. These strategic actions are well documented in the literacy field, most specifically by Fountas & Pinnell (2007), but Liv felt our presentation lacked "teacher words," so she created the following slide to address the need:

> ## PURPOSE OF LIVBITS
> ♥ **Reflection**
> ♥ **Synthesis**
> ♥ **Feedback**

Teachers often snap pictures of this slide. Liv always gives me a little wink when she sees people's phones go up in our presentations. It confirms to her how powerful her work is when coupled with words teachers can directly connect to their own practice. Liv likes to say she creates slides that are meant to go viral, and if that's not proof of purpose, I am not sure what is.

Viral messages are ones that create an intensity—a reaction with the potential for a heartbeep. Many times, people create with the desire to go viral, but this mindset is what Pink would characterize as an extrinsic motivator. It's from the experiences within the creation process—the ones where students are deeply committed to the creation of content and the deepening satisfaction and understanding of their own message for the world—where the potential for impact resides.

And maybe we can rethink the idea of viral just a bit and include Liv's distinction between being famous and being global. Liv would argue her earlier example of the raucous cheering from her school visit helped her define more specifically a key purpose in her LivBit work—a "viral idea" in her LivBit life—one that has motivated and influenced her subsequent creations.

As we close this chapter, I would be remiss if I didn't relate how Liv saw her purpose at the beginning of her LivBit journey.

Liv began creating videos after she experienced bullying in second grade. If I'm completely transparent, I wanted a distraction for her. I knew Liv was an avid reader, and I figured she'd seen many kid-created videos from a research project I was leading called the Selfie Center. These videos were short selfie-style video "bits" of students thinking about their reading. These videos were an early effort on my part to encourage teachers to document student reflection using technology. All of this research was done well before there were the incredible apps we have now to document student thinking using video.

Liv was fascinated by the research and would spend hours reviewing video clips with me. She often begged to create her own videos, and up until that point, I hadn't actively encouraged her to try it. It was out of desperation I allowed Liv to make her first video, as a way for her to find her voice and confidence again.

From her first LivBit video, Liv demonstrated an incredible sense of autonomy, mastery, and purpose. She created the catchy ending that has come to define her work: "Keep reading, keep thinking, and keep watching LivBits for more ideas about your books." When I posted it to my Instagram account, Liv's work immediately resonated with an audience outside of our family, and followers began asking for more videos. A few months into creating LivBits, I brought Liv to ITSE in Denver, CO. It was her first conference ever, and I gave her fifteen minutes to talk about her project. She captivated the audience. Liv

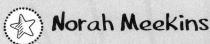

Norah Meekins

@norahchristine.danser: Creative Communicator

Norah uses Instagram to share her passion for ballet. What I love about Norah's work is that it's based on a specific theme, so we get to dive deep into her world. It's so awesome to see how she curates inspiring ballet content.

I also love how Norah thinks about purpose as "using your God-given talents . . . to try to make the world a better place . . . and help others strive for excellence and live without a fear of failure."

Norah aims to share dance-related learning opportunities by promoting a non-profit organization that she belongs to called Ballet in the City. As an ambassador, she fundraises, participates in photo shoots for ballet functions, and works to expose more kids to the arts, especially ballet.

Norah loves the feeling of "passing on those positive vibes," when she sees an encouraging Instagram post. Two of her favorite trailblazing ballerinas to follow are Misty Copeland and Ingrid Silva. When Norah posts on Instagram, her biggest hope is for people to learn that "it is okay to not be perfect because we are all still growing." And, of course, Norah would love to inspire more kids to try ballet!

Norah's hashtag for the world:
#HardWorkandDeterminationResultsinGrowth

knew from that moment onward, her work meant something bigger than we could have imagined.

Liv didn't start her video creation journey by telling her bullying story first; instead she created from a place of comfort—her love of reading. This bookish start allowed her to gain traction around her creation process and also allowed her to consider how to capture messages her audience would enjoy. Liv has a strong sense of purpose when it comes to messaging and realizes the importance of sharing messages that are hopeful, kind, and true. When children create from a place of passion and purpose—with consideration for audience reaction—they have the opportunity to see their digital citizenship and all its possibilities.

Chapter Three

Digital Authenticity

> Have you ever thought about the power of authentic student voice in digital spaces?

ast year I was a keynote speaker at a major tech conference. It was a conference I had anticipated for a long time, because I got to go back to a state I love and see many people who helped grow my LivBit work. The night before the conference kickoff, there was a special dinner for all of the key conference people, including the keynote speakers. I sat at the big long table sort of pinching myself. I felt so proud to be included.

As we were eating, people excitedly connected and talked about lots of things, including the tech projects they were currently working on. Many people shared ideas they had for posts to promote their work and which platforms seemed to give them the most encouragement. Several people thanked me for helping them spread the word about their work and for being a mentor to them in their posts. The feeling in the room was exhilarating!

What happened next is still hard for me to fully understand. The coordinator of the conference looked at the group and interrupted,

"I just always assume it's not Liv that's actually posting, but really it's her mom."

There was an immediate awkward silence. Then people nervously began eating whatever was in front of them. My mum looked at me from across the table, her eyes intently signaling "it's OK." She added a wink and a smile for extra reassurance.

In the moment after that comment was made, I swallowed a lot more than the bread I was eating—I swallowed the hurt I felt from an adult I admired making assumptions about my authenticity online. The truth is, lots of people don't truly believe in student voice, even if they invite you to their conference to be a keynote speaker.

My mum and I talked later that night about the idea of authenticity, and she explained that maybe I'm the one to show this coordinator just how authentic student voice can be.

I view all the work I do online as an opportunity to build relationships. It can be hard to understand who is real online and who isn't; who is supportive and who is lurking; who feels jealousy and who feels genuine happiness when you've accomplished something big. Social media puts a magnifying glass on all these things. My mum and I have talked a lot about having an authentic voice online, and she encourages me to find people whose voices I admire. I study those voices. I think about what their message is for the world. Then I try to develop my own voice so people will recognize me by how I sound. In other words, how I sound if I'm having dinner with you will match how I sound if I'm posting about my passions.

I hope as you read this chapter, you'll consider a few important ideas about authenticity and digital experiences. First, my mum and I present authenticity in a super purposeful way. We want you to think, "Yes! That's a real kid with a real message!" I'll let my mum explain more about this. Next, we hope you consider how passion can drive what kids create and share online. You have to allow kid-driven passions into classroom spaces, because those passions are the messages kids can share with the world. And finally, kids can create incredible content. Give them a chance. Believe they did

Connection to the ISTE Standards

Educator Standard 3: Citizen

Educators inspire students to positively contribute to and responsibly participate in the digital world. Educators:

a. Create experiences for learners to make positive, socially responsible contributions and exhibit empathetic behavior online that build relationships and community.

b. Establish a learning culture that promotes curiosity and critical examination of online resources and fosters digital literacy and media fluency.

c. Mentor students in the safe, legal and ethical practices with digital tools and the protection of intellectual rights and property.

d. Model and promote management of personal data and digital identity and protect student data privacy.

Educator Standard 6: Facilitator

Educators facilitate learning with technology to support student achievement of the ISTE Standards for Students. Educators:

a. Foster a culture where students take ownership of their learning goals and outcomes in both independent and group settings.

b. Manage the use of technology and student learning strategies in digital platforms, virtual environments, hands-on makerspaces or in the field.

c. Create learning opportunities that challenge students to use a design process and computational thinking to innovate and solve problems.

d. Model and nurture creativity and creative expression to communicate ideas, knowledge or connections.

the work when you see it. Tell them you are proud of the great things they are doing, and then let them hear it from an audience bigger than just your classroom.

Acknowledging Authentic Student Voice

Liv's story asks us to remember that it's not just about giving student voice a seat at the table; it's about believing what's behind the message. In some ways, I imagine this conference coordinator must have felt a sort of Ozian understanding of what Liv creates. On the one hand, she saw online the positivity Liv's work generates, and she wanted her conference to have that experience. On the other hand, she clearly doubted a kid could pull all that off—there had to be someone "behind the curtain" helping her. Maybe, as we sat at that dinner, she began to realize just how authentic Liv's work truly is, and hopefully her own thinking about student voice grew.

It's important to navigate online spaces with an eye for authenticity, even if social media platforms create an ever-changing landscape of what this might mean. And, unfortunately, it's true there are instances when a kid becomes the "face" of a cause, when an adult actually creates and posts the content. Liv is often compared to several of these kids. At the beginning of her LivBit journey, she would privately try to inform people why her work was different from those examples. As consumers of information, we are often drawn to the "cute kid" and forget to consider whether or not they are really creators of the content. As teachers, we are working hard to help children discern what is authentic and how to identify whether research is accurate. Navigating information, causes, and movements online, no matter how it's packaged, should be no different.

In her school visit keynote speeches, Liv always shares her ideas about being authentic. She also shares that one of the best compliments she can get is when she meets a follower face to face and they say, "You are *just* like you are on your LivBits!"

If you interact with Liv frequently online, she will remember you. If she finds out you might be at a conference she is attending or she's near the town or city you live in, she's excited about the possibility of seeing you. In fact, she will blow up your profile picture so that she can see what you look like, and then look for you in a crowd of people.

Liv assumes if you've interacted together a lot online, you'd want to interact face to face.

The adults in her life often refer to her work online as her "digital life," but Liv doesn't see her work online as anything other than her life. She doesn't separate it into digital and real. Liv's mindset gives us a key consideration for fostering a global sense of self, leadership among peers, and activism online.

Connected Learning Matters

Connected learning opportunities help students develop key understandings about the world around them. Liv's work provides a model for global understanding, how this can lead to social action, and how students develop a deeper sense of empathy and kindness from interacting with the world. Children can't become changemakers if they aren't empowered to think beyond their own community. Liv's online sense of agency serves as an example of maximizing opportunities, developing a powerful voice, and making global connections that deepen her compassion for people and the world.

After every single school visit, Liv is flooded with messages through her website from the children she meets. The majority of the messages are like the one shown here: true admiration and awe for what she does, often coupled with a desire from the messenger to do it too.

Comment

Hi Olivia, I loved when you came and did a speech at Richardson Elementary. I think you story is so powerful. I didn't know about you before you came and boy am I glad you came. You are such a motivational person. I would like to know a few things. Does your family have to pay for all your flights in order to travel? I can't belive how amazingly you spoke infront of everyone, that must be hard. I like to donate stuff on my birthday to hospitals this year I want to do something like you. Being kind is the best feeling in the world. I love your Livbits sooooo much!!! Keep doing awesome!!!?? You ROCK, Makenzie

---

It's also true that almost every school visit includes one nasty message through her website. We've come to expect it. Recently a student posted this cruel comment:

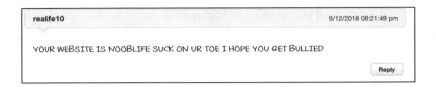

realife10   9/12/2018 08:21:49 pm

YOUR WEBSITE IS NOOBLIFE SUCK ON UR TOE I HOPE YOU GET BULLIED

Reply

Liv has become more and more adept at handling that kind of feedback. Although it's still hurtful, her reactions have become more thoughtful. As she often says in keynotes, "Going through hard experiences can help you see the world with more empathy." She now shrugs with a sigh and adds, "We've got a lot more work to do."

However, Liv has a harder time with negative comments when they're on social media platforms where the audience is much wider. Next we'll share several techniques we've developed to help Liv understand how to safely navigate these situations.

Leaning On Your Digital Crew

Liv has a digital crew she calls on when she needs help on social media platforms. The idea for the crew was very intentional and came out of a "Mr. Roger's mindset." I wanted her to look for the helpers on these platforms. It was impossible for me to always be right there when Liv was online, but I knew there were plenty of other people who cared about Liv and would look out for her, if needed. Initially, her digital crew consisted of people she knew in her everyday life, but as she began doing more and more work online, and started using the hashtag #DigitalCrew, people began asking how they could help. Before we knew it, Liv had dozens and dozens of people asking to be part of her crew.

DIGITAL CREW

A group of people online I can tag if the social media waters get rough. They are my FIRST RESPONDERS if someone is a goober to me.

Liv wishes every child had a digital crew to help them navigate being online. In her experience, she has found so many incredible helpers—people who have become true champions of her work.

One of these champions has supported Liv's work since the very beginning. Liv met @HelentheShark after deciding she needed to follow every tagged OCEARCH shark on Twitter. Their interactions extended Liv's deep love for shark conservation and shark information, and Helen quickly fell in love with Liv's shark-girl enthusiasm. In true Liv fashion, she created a special hashtag for Helen and began curating their interactions with #GuardianShark. In Liv's opinion, every child deserves to have a guardian shark.

There have been many times when Helen has circled the waters for Liv, protecting and defending her when needed.

#SharkGuardian in ACTION

These experiences have helped Liv understand that being a change-maker means understanding how your message resonates both positively and negatively.

Block and Bloom

Helen also had a brilliant technique she shared with Liv early on: block and bloom. This technique empowers Liv to disengage from any thread where someone acts aggressively or negatively. The premise of block and bloom is simple: Some people don't deserve your energy or time, so block them in order to keep blooming. Liv knows to tag her crew and let them take care of the situation.

There haven't been many times when Liv has had to ask her digital crew to help her out. This is an important fact to consider: In three years' time, Liv has had only four instances on social media platforms when she needed assistance. Each time, the instigator was connected to the teaching field. In one instance, the troublemaker's bio even claimed she was a "digital citizenship expert." We've found that each time someone has come after Liv on a thread, it's because they don't care much about hearing her opinion. This is probably not unlike what she experiences in her day-to-day interactions at school or maybe even at home with her sister and brother. In other words, we spend a lot of time fretting over the possible hazards of social media platforms, when the negative experiences may not be any greater than what is experienced offline.

> Some people will never help you grow your work. Block them, let your digital crew take care of the negativity, and keep on blooming!

After hearing Liv's bullying story, a teacher asked her, "What's worse—bullying in real life or bullying online?" Liv's answer was simple: "It's all real life. It feels terrible to be bullied no matter where it happens." As long as we continue to regard digital spaces as being different from face-to-face interactions, we will miss opportunities for students to develop the empathy needed to be good citizens in any space they frequent.

At a recent parent presentation Liv and I did in New Jersey, an audience member listened intently to Liv share her bullying story. As she listened, she softly cried and clutched a tissue tightly in her fist. It was evident she connected deeply to Liv's experience. Later, the audience member, a mom, approached Liv and complimented her bravery. She went on to share how much she admired Liv's resolve to create something good from something so bad. Liv leaned into the woman's ear and whispered, "I've learned the world cares more than people realize." At this, the woman reached out and embraced Liv in a tight hug, nodding her head in agreement.

So much of what Liv does on and offline is a search for meaning. She looks for people to connect with who will grow her thinking, causes, and ideas. It's true there is more good online than bad. Yes, there are trolls and haters, but Liv has learned how to navigate those situations nimbly, and I imagine she will encounter plenty more challenges as she continues to grow her work. But I am confident she has the skill set to seek help when she needs it—blocking when necessary, and blooming as a result.

Embracing a Digital Conscience

Often when people make a mistake online, someone asks what their grandparents would think if they saw the post. It's very true; grandparent opinion could act as a deterrent for someone engaging in questionable posting. Teacher-author Cris Tovani has been an avid supporter of Liv's work since the beginning of her LivBit journey, and she took this idea one step further by referring to Liv as her "digital conscience." Tovani asserted that she thinks more deeply when she posts because she understands Liv's eyes might see her words.

Liv was intrigued by what she considered a big responsibility—being someone's digital conscience. In order to understand the concept better, she looked up the words *digital* and *conscience*. Then she highlighted the words in each definition she felt were most important. Finally, she created her own definition using the words she highlighted.

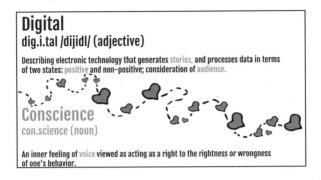

Digital
dig.i.tal /dijidl/ (adjective)

Describing electronic technology that generates stories, and processes data in terms of two states: positive and non–positive; consideration of audience.

Conscience
con.science (noun)

An inner feeling of voice viewed as acting as a right to the rightness or wrongness of one's behavior.

DIGITAL CONSCIENCE

An awareness of how stories are viewed by your audience; a desire to make a positive impact with your voice.

Liv's definition of digital conscience, "an awareness of how stories are viewed by your audience; a desire to make a positive impact with your voice," perfectly encapsulates how we can empower students' awareness online and their sense of responsibility for what they post and create. In other words, an online presence demands a digital conscience.

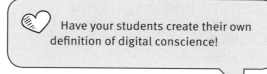

Have your students create their own definition of digital conscience!

It's true that students can also operate in these digital spaces without the knowledge of how powerful the space can be. In her keynote speeches, Liv often uses an example from an exchange in a Twitter chat where a follower quoted Liv's disappointment that only boys have been featured on Discovery Channel's Shark Week. After this tweet came a response from another follower who shared, "YES!! That girl gets social justice and having a voice!" (Mattson, 2016). After reading an archive of the chat, Liv came to me and asked, "What do people mean when they say I 'get' social justice?"

Once Liv learned what this exchange meant, it was as if a fire had been lit inside her, and she went back and examined earlier content to see if there were any other social justice connections. As Pink stated, "When we make progress and get better at something, it is inherently motivating. In order for people to make progress, they have to get feedback and information on how they're doing" (2009). Liv's need to critique and analyze her previous posts creates incredible opportunities for her literate life. She's able to think and create a "meta" analysis of her own work and then take action to grow her message even more deeply.

Understanding and Engaging
Your Audience

It's evident Liv intuitively understands the power of curation from the engagement she receives with her online audience. Nothing makes her more excited than when she posts a new blog and immediately sees red dots on her website's map. The free RevolverMap widget on her site tracks the number of hits her site gets and also identifies the continent, country, and state where viewers are located. If you contact Liv through her website, the same widget also enables her to locate where you sent the message from by the IP address your device carries. RevolverMap then "pins" your location with a red dot on a Google Earth map for Liv to see. For Liv, it's as if those red dot readers are standing at her desk giving her a pat on the back for a job well done. She'll squeal in delight, "There's Pana! And, I think that might be Heather!" as the red dots pop up on the globe indicating a new person is now reading her post. When she's unsure who a dot might represent, she'll ask, "Who do we know in Australia? Who lives in Bangladesh?" Liv sees her content as a way to understand the world, and when the world speaks back, even if it's a tiny dot on the map, she immediately tries to figure out the connection.

Liv's global blogging connections show the power of others helping us become ourselves (Vygotsky, 1978). Her engagement and wonder motivate her to create more content, get more feedback, and grow her understanding of herself as a writer. According to Vygotsky (1978), humans use tools that develop from a culture, such as speech and writing, to mediate their social environments. Liv leverages the tremendous impact of her red-dotted audience to create more engaging and powerful blog posts, while also creating her own authentic story for the world.

At a recent conference, I attended a panel on student voice. An audience member asked the panel their opinions of student use of filters on photos. He wondered if the use of filters created a lack of authenticity on platforms where photos are shared. There were several comments from the audience, most confirming filters were bad. Later, when we were having dinner, Liv circled back to the question asked at the panel and wondered why adults don't see the value of filtered photos, because in her opinion they help create a more interesting story. This juxtaposition of views suggests the challenge for adults to understand student agency online. If we view filters as bad and students view them as a way to amplify good, there needs to be more dialogue around developing a better understanding of what students see and how they see it.

Liv's experiences online have always been driven by her. Even in the beginning when she was first learning how to navigate the platforms she was on, Liv would come to me knowing what she wanted to post. In other words, I wasn't saying to her, "Liv, post this . . . and now post this." Her thinking and excitement about her LivBit work drove the types of posts she would make. But another driving force in her ability to make decisions about her work was her burgeoning sense of audience and the power they had to guide her story.

Liv has an incredible visual she often uses in her presentations to define authenticity. It's an image from her Tutu Project (she's an accomplished ballerina and has me take pictures for the fundraiser in every city she visits). She always shares, "Your posts define who we are and are a mirror to the world." I like deconstructing Liv's visual and her message even more by adding how powerful it is to truly see yourself. There Liv is, gazing at her own image, standing firmly in a

Your posts are a MIRROR to the world.

place where her hands come together and her shadow extends into the mirror; it's as if she is able to completely see what the world sees, and in doing so, she understands just what being authentic means.

Maybe Liv's simple definition of authenticity is all we need: Who you are online should be who you are offline.

 # Matt Soeth and Kim Karr

@ICanHelp: Digital Citizens

\#ICANHELP is one of my favorite organizations, because it empowers students to create change in digital spaces and use social media positively. The work this organization does is truly a #KidsCanTeachUs model.

My friends Matt Soeth and Kim Karr founded #ICANHELP to encourage students to be "agents of change in digital spaces." They believe students can be the "first responders" to negativity online. I agree! And they are right, we have the power to help each other by reporting, blocking, and telling an adult. I love their mission to create powerful and positive spaces for students to share their stories. #ICANHELP has helped kids like me become "active monitors" of social media, working to remove and address online impersonation, bullying, and harassment.

Matt believes students inspire the #ICANHELP work on every level. As he told me, "Everyone is different and every situation is different, but each person has the power to do something in order to HELP. This is where the hashtag started, as a symbol of support online."

Each year, the organization recognizes students who are making a difference online during their #Digital4Good Day—a celebration bringing industry and youth together to have bigger conversations about building positive social media campaigns and the user experience. As a participant, I can say how mind-blowing it was to learn about all the different ways kids are making such a difference in their online and offline communities.

It's exciting to be connected to an organization who cares so deeply about changing false assumptions about kids and social media.

#ICANHELP's hashtags for the world:

- #ICANHELP
- #IWILLHELP
- #IDIDHELP
- #Digital4Good

Chapter Four

Digital Creation

Did you know creating content online helps kids feel connected to the world?

Kids love to create! I don't think I've ever met a kid who didn't have a desire to create cool things reflecting their passions. If kids have the opportunity to use tech tools as part of the creation process, they can share their work in really powerful ways. We need time to create things we love, access to tools that will help us create in interesting ways, and opportunities to share our creations with a global audience. The global part doesn't have to start immediately. Sharing can first start in a classroom partnership, then grow to a small group, then a whole group, then class to class, then class to school, and last but not least, class to world. But from the beginning of the creation process, kids can have the world in their mind's eye.

It's a very empowering feeling to know the world cares about your work. It's like a great big hug that you'll never forget.

If I think about my own family as an example, I can share my ideas about both my big brother, Quinn, and my little sister, Charlotte. Because my mum will be sharing about Charlotte's work for the

> # Kids are NATURAL creators
> ## They NEED:
> ### Time ⏰
> ### Access 🔑
> ### Sharing Opportunities ⌥

world in a later chapter, I'd love to share what I've learned about creation from my brother, Quinn.

Quinn loves to build with LEGOS. In fact, he'll spend hours with a new box that has thousands of little pieces to put together, and he'll barely even move until he's figured everything out. My mum says LEGOs are Quinn's kryptonite; he just can't resist them. If there's a LEGO in the room, it sends a signal to Quinn's brain that it needs to be put together.

A few summers ago, a friend gave Quinn a big tub filled with random LEGO pieces. Quinn has such an incredible brain for seeing how LEGO pieces go together, he looked into the tub and immediately knew it held rare pieces for a Harry Potter Hogwarts castle. Quinn spent days organizing the pieces, putting them together, and making a list of what was missing. Then he and my dad searched through LEGO bins Quinn already had and found similar pieces that would substitute nicely for what was missing from the Hogwarts castle. It was amazing to see Quinn work on this; he was designing and problem-solving and completely dedicated to rebuilding the castle no matter what was missing. He was in full LEGO creation mode, and he was so motivated and happy.

Throughout the building process, Quinn documented his work by taking pictures with an iPad. He loved scrolling through all the pictures and talking about the building process. Even though I'm

not much of a LEGO builder, I enjoyed hearing Quinn talk about his castle because it reminded me of the work I do in Minecraft.

Quinn also did loads of research about his castle design. When he was unsure what was missing, he'd pore over old LEGO guides to see if he could figure out what he needed. He took screenshots and zoomed in on castle photos he found online. He also brought in some of his own ingenuity by considering how to add a few robotic parts into the castle design, like a pulley that carries a water bucket up the side of the tower.

Every bit of his focus was on creating the castle as if it was new out of the box—or better.

That's what using tech to create around your passions can do for you. You can document, design, problem-solve, and connect across platforms in ways that help you develop the creative side of your brain. Once you've experienced this, you begin to wish for more opportunities to create. The tech doesn't have to be fancy either. It can be as simple as having the opportunity to create a picture stream, or researching and studying documents you find online, or using an old robot part from another toy in a new and interesting way.

When I think of Quinn and his castle, I feel like I can see a bit of his future. It's like imagining how his love of designing and building might help him actually build another castle someday, one that he might invite me to for dinner.

And I hope you haven't missed this detail: Quinn's story started out just between us and now it's for the world, because it's here in this book. There are powerful examples of kid creation everywhere if we just take a minute to notice.

Let Passions Drive Creation

Creation that's premised on kid passion can give us a glimpse into a student's future. Liv's apt description of Quinn's purposeful, resourceful, and focused dedication to his castle project reminds me of

Connection to the ISTE Standards

Educator Standard 2: Leader

Educators seek out opportunities for leadership to support student empowerment and success and to improve teaching and learning. Educators:

a. Shape, advance and accelerate a shared vision for empowered learning with technology by engaging with education stakeholders.

b. Advocate for equitable access to educational technology, digital content and learning opportunities to meet the diverse needs of all students.

c. Model for colleagues the identification, exploration, evaluation, curation and adoption of new digital resources and tools for learning.

Educator Standard 4: Collaborator

Educators dedicate time to collaborate with both colleagues and students to improve practice, discover and share resources and ideas, and solve problems. Educators:

a. Dedicate planning time to collaborate with colleagues to create authentic learning experiences that leverage technology.

b. Collaborate and co-learn with students to discover and use new digital resources and diagnose and troubleshoot technology issues.

c. Use collaborative tools to expand students' authentic, real-world learning experiences by engaging virtually with experts, teams and students, locally and globally.

d. Demonstrate cultural competency when communicating with students, parents and colleagues and interact with them as co-collaborators in student learning.

---

what Csikszentmihalyi (1990) refers to as "flow"—a feeling of intense concentration and enjoyment people experience when they work on a satisfying task. When kids create, they can find their flow much quicker when it comes from a place of passion; it's what we often refer to as our "happy place." This is true for adults too. Csikszentmihalyi (1996) asserts adults need to be mindful of the playful side of creativity; the most creative people tend to be those who can hyper-focus on the task at hand, while also persevering through challenges. For most people, finding your flow is a lifelong pursuit.

Liv's ability to connect with incredible authors, scientists, ballerinas—experts who extend her passions—helps her contextualize her interests into real-world experiences. November (2012) asserts that we have a responsibility to students to help them develop networks that support their lifelong learning. Just as Liv can imagine Quinn's pursuits in the future, her own connectedness to a network of experts allows Liv to imagine her own future, too.

This chapter is an invitation for you to consider the content Liv creates as both an example and catalyst for your own classroom. Liv's creations are original only in the sense that they reflect her own passions and her networks that grow them. Your classroom can serve as a platform for student passions and networking.

Seeing More Clearly

Recently, I've had some eye-related issues, which caused me to spend a lot of time with my eye doctor. In my initial visits, I hoped for a simple diagnosis of the problem, or a remedy that would get me quickly out of the office and back into my everyday routine. Unfortunately, my vision issues are quite complicated, so quick visits weren't always in the cards for me. In order to ease my anxiety, I began to focus on the tools my doctor used in my visits. How did she understand my eye condition? Which tools were most important?

At almost all of my visits, my doctor used the most common tool—the phoropter. This tool measures the way the eyes work together, as well as the refractive errors of the eyes. More than likely, you've had experience with this tool if I remind you of the question the doctor asks as she uses it: "What's clearer . . . one or two?" The doctor uses your feedback to make adjustments to the lenses you are looking through.

The goal is to measure the unique differences in the vision of both eyes and to fine-tune your vision so whatever treatment you need, you enjoy clearer vision.

The thought process I used to ease my own anxiety during my eye appointments can be instructive in easing any anxiety we might feel as we consider tech tools, platforms for sharing, and delving deeper into how to create authentic networks for your students.

Just as the phoropter measures the unique differences in my eyes, I am continually measuring my own understanding of tech tools and experiences with Liv's. I've had to trust myself to follow Liv's lead, and because we've developed such a strong network of capable and caring others—her digital crew—she's learned to make sense of the complexity of the world in ways I would have doubted if I didn't see it happening. Liv simply says her work has helped her "love the world more," and this is certainly the case. But more specifically, she sees the human side of technology—and this understanding empowers the kinds of decisions she makes online. She creates thinking about "her people," and this helps her see a bigger purpose for her work. Put simply, people depend on Liv, and she depends on them. It's as if when she's holding the tech, she sees the world right in the palm of her hands.

There will always be differences between how you and your students see technology. I've learned the clearest vision requires us to be understanding and open-minded. We must focus on where students' creations can take them and allow for the nuances that their particular journey will contain. I go back to the questions I asked to ease my nerves during my eye doctor visits, though slightly nuanced: How do I understand Liv's experience? Which tools were most important?

As I share Liv's creations here, I hope you imagine first, the general ways she uses technology and that the tech tools are only powerful when they create a clearer picture for thinking and understanding. Next, I hope you consider the value of the nuances in how we envision the work children do online.

Keep Reading! Keep Thinking!

Liv's videos are her most popular piece of content and what started her on this creation journey. Each week, she makes short videos discussing her reading and thinking. They are done in a "selfie" style: She looks straight into the camera, shares her thinking, then leans in and switches off the camera. It's a simple format that doesn't require much practice, and we've found most students feel comfortable and confident trying this style themselves.

Gretchin Aviles's third-grade classroom in New Hampshire analyzed Liv's work and created an anchor chart to help them create their own LivBit-style videos.

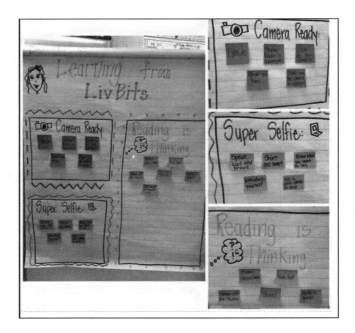

The anchor chart focuses on three categories they noticed in Liv's videos:

- Camera Ready: Smile; show books as examples; look at the camera; show your face; make sure the camera is centered.

- Super Selfie: Introduce yourself; speak loud and proud; know what you want to say; keep it short and sweet; use a catchphrase at the end.

- Reading Is Thinking: Make connections; do a book chat; show off your fluency; invite a guest.

Sticky note tips define the categories (as listed above) and become a powerful reference for students as they get ready to create.

Innovation specialist Pana Asavavatana refers to Liv as a "mentor tech" for her K–2 students in Taiwan because of Liv's ability to talk about the tech decisions she makes while she creates her videos. Her students also analyzed Liv's work and created a plan for their own LivBit-style videos. Asavavatana's anchor chart included an Instagram post of Liv's how-to list for making a catchy LivBit, then a QR code children could use to access all of Liv's videos. Once they did this, the students worked to create a plan for how their videos would unfold, including drafting their own questions about their topics, considering how to hook their audience, and crafting unique catchphrases at the end of their videos. Asavavatana was an early adopter of Liv's work, and her students provided some invaluable feedback that Liv used to strengthen her later videos, most specifically, by slowing down the pace she talked in her videos. Most of Liv's Taiwan collaborators are second language speakers, so Liv's fast-talking style sometimes meant they had to listen multiple times before they understood her message. Their feedback helped Liv learn the power of pacing and how an audience needs time to process what you are sharing.

This back-and-forth reflection process creates an incredible amount of analysis and critique in Liv's creation loop. The empowerment isn't one-sided. Although Liv's work generates powerful considerations for

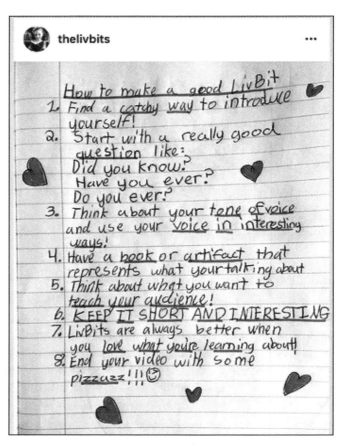

thelivbits

How to make a good LivBit
1. Find a catchy way to introduce yourself!
2. Start with a really good question like:
   Did you know?
   Have you ever?
   Do you ever?
3. Think about your tone of voice and use your voice in interesting ways!
4. Have a book or artifact that represents what your talking about
5. Think about what you want to teach your audience!
6. KEEP IT SHORT AND INTERESTING
7. LivBits are always better when you love what you're learning about!
8. End your video with some pizzazz!!! ☺

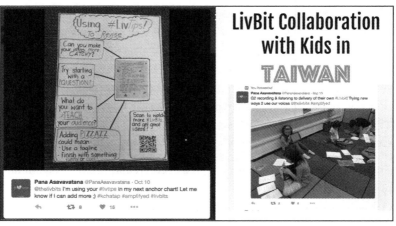

LivBit Collaboration with Kids in TAIWAN

> Every kid can be a mentor tech! Let them create, then ask them to talk about their decisions. BOOM! Mentor tech in action!

students and teachers in their own creation loop, Liv receives candid kid-generated perspective on her work, and this motivates her to create more content they will enjoy.

Principles of Feedback

Although the creation loop is a powerful mechanism that empowers the learner to experiment with new learning stances, it also becomes an important tool for feedback. After observing Liv's impact on students and teachers, and their impact on her, I identified four principles of feedback impacting the learner. Unpacking these feedback principles is essential if teachers want to encourage students to be effective givers and receivers of feedback.

The most effective feedback is continuous

In order for students to understand how to use reflection as part of the learning process, feedback has to happen. As Liv considered the feedback from her peers in Taiwan about the speedy pace of her talking, she began to examine other elements of her fluency, like pausing, intonation, rhythm—the prosody of her speech. Nichols (2006) suggests purposeful talk is the motivation for students to construct ideas and "visions of possibility" for themselves and each other. It's clear in Liv's process, the feedback from the purposeful talk became the possible next steps for her as a learner in the creation loop.

Feedback is co-constructed

This positions the learner in a very powerful role. They can either choose to use the feedback or ignore it; choose to refine their ideas or keep them the same; choose to complicate their learning goal or stay consistent with how they initially began the process. In Liv's case, she needed to choose to slow down her talk or to keep being speedy and risk losing the opportunity to develop a more purposeful rhythm to her videos where her audience felt more supported.

Feedback offers us the opportunity to see learning that's positioned between the giver and receiver, and it creates opportunities for next steps for each of them. The conversation around the learner's process becomes a tool to strengthen the learning (Vygotsky, 1978). The giver can think about how she might try what Liv has done, and Liv can consider the giver's feedback and grow a specific aspect of her work. The give and take that can happen when feedback begins with a question shows the potential power of how talk can deepen the work (Nichols, 2006). Questions help strengthen the learning for everyone.

Feedback is intended to build confidence

Students receive large amounts of feedback rapidly every day. They have to learn to sift through the feedback to make better sense of how their learning is being perceived by others, while also deciding what their next steps might be. Students also need to know how to make sense of negative feedback, because this type of feedback happens and is often what breaks the learner down. When some learners receive negative feedback, they can't categorize it in a way that helps them know what their next step might be. Instead, they shut down, and the creation loop ends.

This is especially true on social media platforms. Feedback comes rapid fire, and sometimes with no filter. Ideally the learner will calibrate the feedback sources. For example, Liv asks herself: Is this feedback meant to grow my thinking in a useful way? Is this source someone who uses my work respectfully? Can I count on this person in more than just this instance to grow my work with me?

It is crucial teachers consider how feedback is framed, especially when today's students will always experience feedback in diverse, dynamic learning environments. The most effective feedback Liv receives is in the form of a question. Students and teachers asking about her creation process helps her articulate the decisions she makes as a learner. Most of the time, the questions Liv receives are also incredibly specific: Why are your videos so short? Do you use a script? How did you think of your catchphrase? How do you decide what book you're going to talk about? Why do you always wear a message shirt? The questions give Liv a glimpse into the arc of understanding her work generates—she can understand what stands out to her audience, and maybe these aren't things she considered much while she was creating her LivBit videos.

Helping students deconstruct feedback can help them develop more specific questions as they learn new skills or take risks as learners. So often, children tap out of the feedback process because they feel the feedback doesn't grow who they see themselves to be, creating insecurities in their sense of self that prevents risk-taking. Let's face it, receiving feedback can make us feel insecure, but if teachers help contextualize the feedback and explicitly model the power of a positive stance, then students can emerge more confident in their abilities.

Feedback adds dimensions to your thinking

Feedback should be timely, and it doesn't have to be complicated. Asking questions as the learner is engaged in the creation loop can help students refine and sharpen their thinking. At this phase of the creation loop (see page 20), encouraging self-assessment—even through a simple emoji exit slip—can help the students track their thinking and offer opportunities for them to deepen their understanding.

Teachers who make feedback a priority encourage kids to add dimensions to their thinking, and Liv's work is an excellent example of this. She first began creating videos and from the feedback those videos generated, she saw opportunities for more content creation—eventually becoming a blogger, podcaster, and accomplished public speaker.

EMOJI EXIT SLIP

Circle how you're feeling after today's work

Liv describes her creation process as a series of nesting dolls—the largest representing her LivBit videos, then each smaller doll representing her other creations. If children are encouraged to create from a passion-filled place, the dimensions they add to their thinking are awe-inspiring. The next doll Liv can add to her nesting doll metaphor will include becoming a published author—it's such an incredible accomplishment, I still have to pinch myself. Each step Liv has taken as a creator has shown me how powerful it is when children add dimensions to their thinking by trying out new creation modalities.

 Feedback should be inspiring or affirming! Ask more questions to get more understanding!

The KidLit Show

The LivBit videos have led to some unbelievable opportunities for Liv, including the chance to have her own podcast, called *The KidLit Show*, on Pinna, a subscription-based audio app that streams podcasts, audiobooks, and music for kids.

This is an example of how one creation can lead to another—maybe one you never imagined.

Produced by a company in Brooklyn, New York, the concept for Liv's show was developed around her love of books and talking. Each episode is themed around a big idea drawn from the featured book in the episode, with Liv interviewing the author(s) about their writing process, book connections, and (in true Liv-fashion), thoughts they have about life. The show is lively, fun, and absolutely entertaining for anyone who loves to listen to podcasts.

Liv jumped into this opportunity with no previous experience interviewing; one characteristic of her LivBit videos is that she rarely, if ever, lets anyone featured in the video say more than one small part of her catchphrase "keep thinking." The person driving all the talk in a LivBit video is Liv, and her audience has come to depend on this certainty—a fact, I think, that endears her more deeply to them.

But a podcast interviewing authors required a whole new set of considerations for Liv as a creator. First, she had to write her own questions, and this meant she had to know the authors' books really well, preferably the entire body of their work, so she could ask deeper, more specific craft questions. Most of the authors Liv interviewed on the show were from connections she'd already established through her LivBit work, but a few were ones in partnership with Pinna, so this meant Liv had to read their books and create questions around stories, topics, or genres that may not have been on her radar.

One of Liv's absolute strengths is her ability to talk extemporaneously in her LivBit videos. Probably the number one question Liv is asked about her videos is if she writes a script for them. She always answers in a resounding, "NO!" Liv's talk is based on her passion for the book or idea, and because of this, she has so much to say—most of the time too much! Liv verbally rehearses what she wants to say, and she talks out her message. Her videos always follow a predictable structure: 1) greeting, 2) question, 3) synthesis of message, 4) takeaway, and 5) catchphrase ending. Liv is always very mindful of timing, and she knows her best videos are 60 to 80 seconds. After creating more than 200 videos, she understands the power of style, message, and brevity. Most children don't need a script once they gain the confidence around their ideas and the tools used to share them.

Talk on a podcast is a very different kind of talk, and Liv had to learn the art of give and take in a conversation, how to be fully present in the discussion, and how to genuinely build on an idea or thought shared. She worked so hard on this, and her growth astounded me.

Liv also wrote large portions of her scripts before she would begin taping with the author. She created a Liv's List (books grouped around a theme or topic) for each interview and crafted questions for her live interviews with "kids on the street." She had to master the use of equipment she'd never seen or used before and consider the best way to use her voice, because in a podcast, she couldn't use body language, like shaking her head. All of these requirements came in a short six-week taping season, and she pulled it off because her LivBit work had given her such a strong foundation and the confidence to shine.

Not only did she get to speak to such giants of the writing world as Peter Reynolds, Sean Qualls, and Selina Alko, but Liv also experienced some absolutely authentic learning moments and absorbed some incredible life lessons. Kate DiCamillo shared with Liv how she created her characters by learning how to pay more attention to people and becoming "a careful observer of humanity." Liv tucked that idea immediately inside her heart. Booki Vivat talked to Liv about how she grew her writing identity and advised, "Do not discredit your creative work." Liv has clutched that idea all the way through the writing of this book—and I have too!

If we give children opportunities to create and hone the skills they feel are meaningful, they can easily transfer these skills from one creative process to the next. The ultimate goal is for the student to be able to apply their knowledge and skills inside and outside of the classroom, specifically to new cases, and most especially for them to carry this knowledge and skill to digital platforms where the transference is critical.

In your classrooms, we hope you'll consider having students listen to different types of podcasts. Ask them to focus on how the host gets the guest to talk, and then give them the opportunity to listen to their own voices as they interview someone important to them. Free podcasting apps, such as Anchor and Spreaker, make it easy for children to give podcasting a try. Likewise, SoundCloud and other free hosting sites make sharing their podcasts with a wider audience easier.

The KidLit Show

The Show About Science

Teaching kids how to produce a podcast around their interests is a powerful way to for them to craft narratives and consider what makes a good story. They can practice and analyze various interviewing techniques and learn the production decisions needed to create an interesting listening experience in the podcast. Preparing students by listening to and analyzing other podcasts, such as *The KidLit Show*, *StoryCorps*, or *The Show About Science*, can help your students

StoryCorps

Favorite Podcasts: *The KidLit Show*, *The Show About Science*, *The Show About Politics*, *Wow in the World*, and *Story Pirates*.

Favorite Free Apps for Creating a Podcast: Anchor and Spreaker.

Host your podcast for free on SoundCloud.

consider the various design elements that come into play when creating their own show.

Liv's podcast work added a new purpose to her creative process and an incredible new dimension to her learning. Without her original LivBit video creation, this opportunity would have never happened.

Liv's Lists

Some of my favorite pieces of content Liv creates are her Liv's Lists. These came about very organically. Teachers and students were constantly asking her for book recommendations, often around themes. As she recognized the value of this content and found herself duplicating it, it dawned on her: A list would be a great way to share

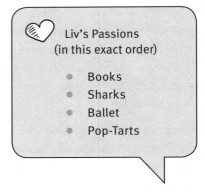

Liv's Passions
(in this exact order)

- Books
- Sharks
- Ballet
- Pop-Tarts

lots of books with students and teachers, and so began Liv's Lists. She has always loved going to the library and taking out piles of books and exploring new genres and themes. Now she does this with her lists in mind. When she shares a new Liv's List online, she gets excited to see an author comment on it or like it. Liv feels proud when she can pair together good books for other children.

Becoming Inspired Through Someone's Story

Several times Liv has posted a Liv's List and received feedback she never expected. This happened recently, when I bought her *Anne Frank: The Diary of a Young Girl* (1993). Liv devoured the book in one night, and it inspired her to make a Liv's List in honor of International Holocaust Remembrance Day.

As she read, Liv felt connected to Anne; she was Dutch like Liv and had a powerful story to share with the world. Liv shared that there were times while she was reading the book when she had to remind herself to breathe. She said she felt Anne's words inside her heart so deeply, it gave her a kind of heartbeep she'd never had before. As soon as she finished the book, she wanted to know more about the history of that time, understand other people's perspectives, and explore the new feelings (heartbeeps) that came from trying to figure out something so massively tragic. Liv carried that emotion into the work she did reading books for her Liv's List. She felt like Anne was depending on her and guiding her.

Olivia Van Ledtje @thelivbits · Jan 29, 2018

My mum bought me the diary of #AnneFrank. I read it in 1 night. I stayed up thinking about the 🌏 Words can change you. "Although I'm only fourteen, I know quite well what I want, I know who is right and who is wrong. I have my opinions, my own ideas." #KidsCanTeachUs #LivsList

After she posted the list, the series of tweets that followed were so powerful. First, people began sharing it, and then readers commented about how personal this list was for them—how it reminded them of people they loved who had suffered during that time. Liv never knew much about the Holocaust before she read Anne's story, and by creating the list she wanted to show how much a person's story can stay with you, move you, and inspire you to take action. The creation also encouraged people to share moving memories of their lives Liv would have otherwise never known.

 You can be carefully prepared but still share your thinking extemporaneously! Try it! You just might love it!

Shark Love

One of Liv's biggest passions beyond books is her love of sharks. So, it makes sense that many students and teachers want her recommendations for the best shark books. The very first Liv's List she created was around her favorite shark books, and she released it during Shark Week.

The enthusiastic feedback Liv received made her think deeply about her desire to do more for sharks and shark conservation.

Team Genie

Liv's passion for sharks began in second grade when she read a biography about a shark scientist called *Shark Lady: True Adventures of Eugenie Clark* (2017), by Ann McGovern. She was immediately drawn to this brave woman who fell in love with sharks as a young girl and never stopped working to change the false public perception that sharks are vicious killers. My husband read online about the Gills Club, an organization designed to encourage girls' passions for sharks, signed up Liv, and her shark journey began.

After a year of tweeting about sharks, her friends on Twitter always had their eyes open for interesting opportunities for Liv to expand her knowledge and passion. One day, a teacher tweeted to Liv about Heather Lang's new picture book biography *Swimming with Sharks: The Daring Discoveries of Eugenie Clark* (2016). From the very first tweet connecting Liv to Lang's shark book, there was a spark of excitement for what their future collaborations might hold. Liv hashtagged their connection as #TeamGenie—and the project was born.

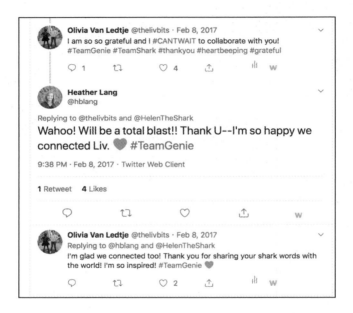

> Have kids hashtag their thinking as a form of synthesis! It doesn't matter the content area, have a place where these hashtags are displayed in your classroom. Each week, have your hashtag crew look for "understanding patterns" across the content areas!

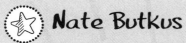

Nate Butkus

@natepodcasts: Knowledge Constructor

I can't think of a better creator for the world than my friend Nate Butkus. Nate's the incredible brain behind *The Show About Science* podcast and his newest podcast, *The Show About Politics*. How cool is that? Nate has TWO podcasts!

Nate loves that he can create something "that sparks change." And it's true Nate's creative process has influenced a lot of important people in the world. He's interviewed lots and lots of scientists about their work, and he's even been on *The Ellen DeGeneres Show*. According to Nate, he is inspired by "people who listen to my podcasts and how they are so supportive . . . and the fact I am really curious."

I like to think of Nate and me as the #KidsCanTeachUs dynamic duo! We both believe in the power of kids teaching and creating for the world. Nate has the same hope as me: "That the world learns that kids can do all the things adults can do, and I hope the world will learn that lesson soon." Me too, Nate! Me too!

I also hope that after reading Nate's Spotlight, you'll get started with a class podcast and even encourage students to create their own podcasts around a passion. Here's what Nate suggests as the best way to get inspiration for your podcast: "I would recommend taking a walk. Yes, a walk. In this walk, look around you. If you see anything you are curious about, then maybe think about making a podcast about it."

> **Nate's Tip:** "The easiest way to start podcasting is to download an app called Spreaker. All you need to do is push this big red button and—bam—you're podcasting!"

Without the social media platform connecting Liv to Lang, she would have never had the network of opportunities that resulted from their Team Genie work, including a shark dissection at The New England Aquarium, where Liv worked alongside women scientists to understand and explore various shark parts. Lang's mutual enthusiasm for educating the public about sharks motivated Liv in many ways. Together, Team Genie also hosted an "Art for Sharks" contest online that garnered global student art pieces and ended with them Skyping the winning student's second-grade classroom in Taiwan, as well as sending shark books to the Malaysian student who was runner-up.

I hope this chapter has shown you how one project or person can spark so many others. There's no end to the possible LivBit videos, podcast interviews, Liv's Lists, Team Genie collaborations, or other ways Liv can (and *will*) connect and share. Not knowing what she will come up with next is half the fun of watching Liv grow as a creator.

Chapter Five

Digital Activism

> Have you have ever considered the power of kids developing an activist stance in their learning?

A big part of my message is that #KidsCanTeachUs. I use this hashtag a lot because it defines what my LivBit work is all about. Lots of times people think that only grown-ups can be the teacher, but I think that you don't have to be an adult to teach others. I can use my website to share important ideas I have. My followers can teach me, and I can teach them. I can even write a book with some advice about kids and tech. How amazing is that?

My mum mentioned in Chapter Four how I learned so much from my podcasting interviews, and how I've carried many of the ideas from those interviews into my life. If I imagine my podcast as a book, in lots of ways those interviews are the lessons in my podcast story. Thinking about *The KidLit Show* this way gives me so many heart-beeps; it's so special that I can use the authors' words and ideas now in my own work. Lots of times, words are the starting point for activism, and when people mark your words as important to them, I don't think there's ever a better feeling.

The most incredible idea I learned was from Kate DiCamillo. I knew the word *humanity* before, but I'd never thought about what it really meant. The way Kate used it to describe her action as a writer, how she looked for other people's humanity, made me think so much about the way I see people. I asked myself, "How do I see humanity?" Then I began thinking about the power of seeing humanity—really looking more, noticing more, and considering more deeply how to understand other people.

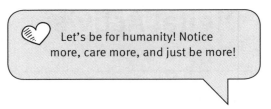

Let's be for humanity! Notice more, care more, and just be more!

I think Kate's advice about noticing humanity is what being an activist is all about: paying attention to people, discovering new things about them, realizing how important everyone is to this world. When we begin to share words to describe all this, we have the power to deepen, change, and grow ideas that matter to the world. That is activism.

Recently, I had an incredible experience as a keynote speaker for Raise Your Voice: A Writing Workshop for Young Activists, hosted by the Teachers College Reading and Writing Project (TCRWP) at Columbia University. The weekend was for kids, and we learned the craft of writing a persuasive speech around a cause we loved (yes, I thought about #TeamGenie and my shark work all weekend long). I was the day two keynote speaker, and just before I was about to deliver my speech, I remember standing in Columbia's Milbank Chapel thinking, there are a lot of incredible people who have shared important words here. Look where LivBits got me. It was a very humbling feeling.

After my keynote, I received a really special email from the TCRWP founding director, Lucy Calkins. I know how important Lucy's work is because my mum has lots of her books in her office, and I've seen her books on my own teachers' bookshelves too. I know Lucy is a very important voice for kids and reading and thinking. Since the very start of LivBits, people would ask me over and over again, "Does Lucy Calkins know about you?" So, when I got to go to TCRWP as a keynote speaker, I thought about Lucy and how people always connected my work to hers.

On the morning of my keynote, I looked up, and there she was: Lucy Calkins. I wasn't nervous to see her or to deliver my keynote; I was just proud to know I finally got to be in the presence of someone who loved words the way I did.

I call myself an activist for words. This means I want people to think more about the words they share. I want people to care about how words shape our humanity.

It was an incredible feeling to know Lucy put aside all of her responsibilities just to hear my words, but I am not surprised. Even before we met in person, our love for words connected us.

So, receiving Lucy's email telling me my words were important was one of my best LivBit moments. When grown-ups you admire are there for you, in words and in actions, it's the best feeling ever.

Connection to the ISTE Standards

Educator Standard 3: Citizen

Educators inspire students to positively contribute to and responsibly participate in the digital world. Educators:

a. Create experiences for learners to make positive, socially responsible contributions and exhibit empathetic behavior online that build relationships and community.

b. Establish a learning culture that promotes curiosity and critical examination of online resources and fosters digital literacy and media fluency.

c. Mentor students in the safe, legal and ethical practices with digital tools and the protection of intellectual rights and property.

d. Model and promote management of personal data and digital identity and protect student data privacy.

Educator Standard 6: Facilitator

Educators facilitate learning with technology to support student achievement of the ISTE Standards for Students. Educators:

a. Foster a culture where students take ownership of their learning goals and outcomes in both independent and group settings.

b. Manage the use of technology and student learning strategies in digital platforms, virtual environments, hands-on makerspaces or in the field.

c. Create learning opportunities that challenge students to use a design process and computational thinking to innovate and solve problems.

d. Model and nurture creativity and creative expression to communicate ideas, knowledge or connections.

I share this story because before LivBits, I never imagined my words would ever be important to people. Now I can see my words through other people. Reading Lucy's email helped me understand this even more.

All kids deserve to feel this kind of understanding, and I hope you help kids find the networks that will help them live out their dreams. I hope you encourage kids to become activists for something, anything they love. I hope you encourage them to share their words and let them know how they can create sparks for humanity.

Activism is really lots of sparks brought together to light the way for others.

One Tiny Step Can Spark Change

Liv crafted an incredibly moving opening to this chapter, so I'll begin with how it feels to be the writer following her lead: intimidating.

Reading Liv's articulation of her own understanding provides an opportunity for introspection. Everything discussed in Chapter Four demonstrates Liv's ability to create something others are inspired by. She uses tech tools to create and spread her message, and her connectedness helps other people get involved in her LivBit mission.

As she shared earlier, Liv sees herself as an activist for words. She loves words, but she also says she's an activist for books. She wants to inspire children to love books more and be the kind of reader who can navigate the world with eyes wide open. This eyes-wide-open view allows Liv to situate her work in the world with the help of technology.

> Being an activist means I think BIGGER than just the things that are important to me; it means I think about what is important to the world!

I'd like to begin with a pivotal story that I think frames nicely the context of technology, activism, and Liv's work. It's a retelling of a blog post Liv wrote called "#Refulgence," but I'll offer my own perspective.

#Refulgence

Traveling with Liv, especially at a conference, can feel a bit like being with a child celebrity. Liv and I joke that people like her because she's a #BookBoss. And this is absolutely true, but more than that, after hearing her speak, the reaction is almost always the same: Listeners feel an immediate need to connect with her one-to-one. It's as if Liv's words have ignited sparks so bright that people have to get closer to her light. And, of course, people also want a selfie—that's a given!

 Be a #BookBoss! Know the power of books and use that power to share messages with the world!

It seems over and over again the same pattern happens. Liv delivers a speech, the audience is genuinely moved by hearing a child with such passion, there's a tremendous buzz on social media platforms about the power of Liv's story, Liv takes a million selfies and throws in a few Boomerang videos for good measure—conference completed.

But at a conference in St. Louis, there was a wrinkle in our normal routine, one that suspended my own understanding of Liv's work and made me first start believing in the idea of her message as a catalyst to spark change.

Michael was our Uber driver from the airport to our hotel. It probably won't surprise anyone to read that Liv loves talking with Uber drivers. Depending on where we are headed, the driver might get an abridged version of her life or, on longer drives, a full detailed account with hardly any pauses.

This was the case in St. Louis. Michael listened intently to Liv share about her LivBit work, his head bobbing in happy concert with her excitement. Michael shared a bit about himself—but only a bit because we had arrived at our hotel carried mostly by Liv's talk. As he took our suitcases from the trunk, Michael wished Liv luck on her keynote, asking once more what day and time it was. I know most people don't hug their Uber drivers, but for some reason when I'm with Liv, this seems like the proper way to part.

Fast-forward three days, and Liv and I are in the ballroom doing last-minute tech and sound checks. Liv is ready to go. I feel a slight tap on my shoulder, and I turn thinking it's the sound guy. To my surprise, it's Michael, our Uber driver!

I stand confused, thinking maybe the conference has ordered our Uber to the airport a bit early, but more confused that by pure coincidence, we'd get the same Uber driver we had on the way into the conference. Without a moment of hesitation, Michael clears my confusion by sharing how he volunteered at the conference for the day, just so he could come to Liv's closing keynote.

Michael brought us to the airport for our return trip to Boston, but this time, he was the one doing most of the excited talking, with Liv and I nodding in agreement. He related his own understanding of Liv's keynote, then offered her one word he felt best described her. Before he shared it though, he warned Liv it might sound like he was swearing at her. This made Liv giggle uncontrollably.

Michael's word describing Liv was *refulgent*, which means to shine brightly.

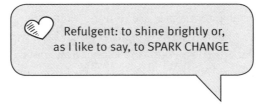

Refulgent: to shine brightly or, as I like to say, to SPARK CHANGE

Notes

Refulgent

to shine brightly ✴
Michael was our Uber driver in St. Louis

Have you ever met someone and thought this is a person I will never forget?

Maybe Michael is like a messenger for someone bigger 😊 like I was meant to meet him to tell me keep working on LivBits because LivBits matters to the world

He has a friendly face that gives people immediate heartbeeps
His smile shows his soul

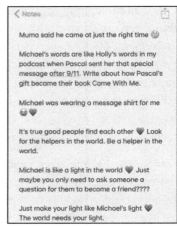

Notes

Muma said he came at just the right time 😊

Michael's words are like Holly's words in my podcast when Pascal sent her that special message after 9/11. Write about how Pascal's gift became their book Come With Me.

Michael was wearing a message shirt for me 😊 💜

It's true good people find each other 💜 Look for the helpers in the world. Be a helper in the world.

Michael is like a light in the world 💜 Just maybe you only need to ask someone a question for them to become a friend????

Just make your light like Michael's light 💜 The world needs your light.

So, this word sat as an invitation to me and Liv as we began thinking about a title for our book—its connection back to Michael and his beautiful vision of my daughter's message is never lost on either of us.

When we boarded the plane to return to Boston, Liv immediately began dictating her ideas for a blog into her iPad. She felt compelled to make sense of this incredible interaction with Michael through her writing. I listened as she whispered her ideas in a note she titled Refulgent.

Liv's blogging process has always involved her iPad and her ability to talk about her thinking. Her note section is a holding place for important ideas she's worried will slip away if she doesn't talk them into her device. Although this isn't an extraordinary example of tech use, it highlights Liv's mindset as a learner. Her iPad notes section is a treasure trove of writing ideas.

Liv's use of her blog to make sense of important experiences draws a global audience to her. After posting that piece, Liv's website received thousands of hits per day. Followers shared how moved they were by this piece and how they hoped Michael saw Liv's words. One classroom of students in Ohio, who are avid readers of Liv's blog posts, sent her touching messages encouraging and lifting Liv's confidence through their comments.

"We can't wait to meet you tomorrow!" –Adrianna (and her entire class!)

"The theme of this blog is so powerful! We could feel it right away!"
–Jessica

"Keep up the good work. I like your blog because it motivates us!" –Tej

"We can't wait to see you tomorrow! It's going to be a fantastic day!" –Alex

"Your blog inspires us to do more for the world." –Jack

"Thank you for making these blogs. This blog is inspiring. It shows that one person you don't know, can make a big difference in your life." –Addie

"Thanks for making these blogs. They make us think, motivate us, and get us reading more!" –Ben

"Your bits make the world better!" –Lily

"You inspired us to be nice and not to be bullies." – Adri

Although these student comments boost Liv's self-esteem as a writer, they also give a glimpse into how Liv's peers view her work. Many children commented that they are inspired by her work, but more importantly, many shared they feel motivated by her words and want to do more for the world.

This comment thread demonstrates the strong desire most students have to make their mark on the world. When we open digital spaces to them and share examples, like Liv's blog, we see how quickly they envision their work being globally relevant.

Liv's excited talk about her work to an Uber driver inspired him to take action and volunteer just to hear her speak. Her message resonated so deeply, he shared an important word with her that now frames so much of the work Liv and I do together. This led to a blog post that inspired many adults and students to think bigger than just their immediate situation, many expressing a desire to do more. This is how activism gets started—one tiny step forward, by someone who takes the risk to lead.

#KidsCanTeachUs

As Liv shared in the opening of this chapter, the #KidsCanTeachUs hashtag represents her LivBit mission. She's curated this hashtag over many years of work and feels excited when she sees other people using it to represent the power of student voice. In Liv's mind, using this hashtag is a digital pat on her back, and most people's use of it has been synonymous with her intentional curation. But two instances involving Liv's ideas around the meaning of this hashtag deepened her understanding more explicitly, adding new iterations to her definition of students teaching others.

First, Liv met a second-grade student who deeply connected to her LivBit video about stereotypes. In the video, Liv explains there's no such thing as "boy stuff" and "girl stuff." Liv created this video out of frustration after looking for shark-related clothes and supplies but finding them only in the boy's section. For this student, however, Liv's message resonated as she was in the process of

Stereotypes

transitioning from boy to girl. I've never witnessed a hug so beautiful as the one between the two of them—the student thanking Liv and whispering, "Your videos help me."

In this same week, Liv met another student who slipped her a special note, telling her how important her #KidsCanTeachUs message was for her.

We learned that Liv's message inspired this fifth grader to use her own voice to improve her living situation and find a foster family for herself and her little brother. I'm certain I cannot capture the emotion of the moment the way Liv did, so here's a small part of her blog about this experience:

> Just as the day was coming to an end, I was greeted in the hallway by a girl who looked about the same age as me, and who I recognized from the morning welcome committee. We had the same caramel color hair and she was wearing a beautiful flower crown

#KidsCanTeachUs

**"I really love kids have a voice...
my voice got me a better family."**
10-year old student

and a message shirt that said, "Girls Rule!" In a small way, it's like she was my reflection...and I'm still thinking about what happened next. My reflection turned to my mum and said, "I really wish I had a mom like you." She said these words softly but purposefully, and her eyes held a small bit of sadness I couldn't really understand. My mum matched her embrace and hugged her deeply. She looked down at her face and whispered, "You just gave my heart a gift. I hope this hug stays with you even after I leave." The girl nodded, then walked away slowly, and at the end of the hallway, she paused and gave us a small wave.

The impact this experience had on Liv was so dramatic, it brought her to tears—tears of compassion, pride, and inspiration to keep finding ways to reach children like this special fifth grader.

Have It All

When Liv hears confusing or concerning messages in the world, she seeks ways to create an understanding, often turning to books. Her Liv's List about Haiti and Africa is an example of this. After reading many books about each country, Liv shared the list online and got immediate and powerful feedback. Followers expressed gratitude to her for creating a resource they could use to counter the negative media information these

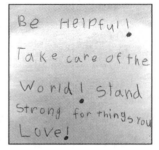

> ♡ I think being an activist comes from creation. Create a story you love. Create your action plan, and make your story matter!

Second grader, Hinsdale, MA

places were receiving. Liv learned her lists could be models around places, people, or themes that are maligned by misinformation in the media. She also learned the power of creating something that provides perspective, and she was determined to create more with this in mind.

Activism is about words and people. Students don't have to march in the streets to be activists. They don't have to be loud or resistant. Activism can sit inside you, waiting to be drawn out. Letting children linger in the beauty of the world is how they find ideas that matter to them. Liv's connectedness has diversified the places she explores, bringing into her sightline causes, places, people, and words she cares about deeply. It's helped her understand humanity.

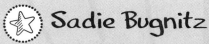

Sadie Bugnitz

@thefeministgazette: Knowledge Constructor

Sadie is a wisdom-filled, fourth-grade activist from Ohio who understands the power of standing up for women's rights. Sadie says an activist is "someone who fights for what they think is not fair and they do something about it." I super love the action Sadie puts into her definition of activist and how her work sparked her school community, her family, and her to participate in the Women's March in Washington, DC.

One of Sadie's first activism projects involved gathering friends who were concerned about inequities between boys and girls at her school. Instead of complaining about the unfairness, Sadie asked, "Why don't we start a club to prove girls and boys are equal?" Sadie's club knew they needed to communicate their ideas about equity and feminism, so they decided a newspaper would be an excellent way to share out important information. With the help of her teacher, Sadie's club was able to use Google Docs to share and write about topics, and the *Feminist Gazette* was born.

Sadie's newspaper has truly sparked a vision for her future activism. She hopes people realize that "girls and boys should be treated equally and that girls are not better than boys and boys are not better than girls." Sadie is currently working on another issue of the *Gazette* with her club, and she hopes to have more opportunities to publish ideas about feminism.

I think the kid-published *Feminist Gazette* should be in the hands of as many people as possible. I'm hoping teachers reading this Spotlight will be inspired to show their students how powerful words are in print and provide more opportunities and platforms for publishing ideas that influence the world. I'm sure Sadie, the feminist, can offer advice on how to make it happen!

Sadie's hashtag for the world: #Feminist

Chapter Six

Digital Exploration

> Have you ever thought about the power of being a global learner?

’ve noticed sometimes grown-ups make tech tools look awkward. For example, have you ever watched a grown-up take a selfie with her phone? My mum shared in Chapter Two the many decisions a selfie taker makes, and now I'm going to explain how a kid sees a grown-up making those decisions.

The first thing I notice is that the selfie taker moves her head in funny ways. Next, she lifts her chin lots of times, turning her face side to side. Then she asks the same question most other grown-ups ask: "Where should I be looking again?"

And then there's a final step. It's when the grown-up actually has to push the button to take the picture. This is usually the most awkward step in the entire process. I've seen some grown-ups reach forward and press the button with their free hand. I've seen people trying to stretch their thumbs in really painful ways. I've seen grown-ups almost drop their phones as they try to snap the selfie, and that

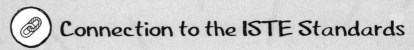

Connection to the ISTE Standards

Educator Standard 1: Learner

Educators continually improve their practice by learning from and with others and exploring proven and promising practices that leverage technology to improve student learning. Educators:

a. Set professional learning goals to explore and apply pedagogical approaches made possible by technology and reflect on their effectiveness.

b. Pursue professional interests by creating and actively participating in local and global learning networks.

c. Stay current with research that supports improved student learning outcomes, including findings from the learning sciences.

Educator Standard 7: Analyst

Educators understand and use data to drive their instruction and support students in achieving their learning goals. Educators:

a. Provide alternative ways for students to demonstrate competency and reflect on their learning using technology.

b. Use technology to design and implement a variety of formative and summative assessments that accommodate learner needs, provide timely feedback to students and inform instruction.

c. Use assessment data to guide progress and communicate with students, parents and education stakeholders to build student self-direction.

means they have to start all over again because now the light is bad and their extra chin is showing.

Most phones have a tiny button right on the side that doesn't require any sort of contortion with your hands or fingers. It's the perfect selfie-taking button. I've found so many grown-ups who don't even know it exists. I always feel so happy when I can help a grown-up take a successful selfie. That's one of my responsibilities as a mentor tech.

Although I know I've helped lots of grown-ups with understanding the power of tools, there are so many ways grown-ups have helped me, too. In this chapter, my mum will discuss the power of my global connections and how being a connected learner helps me explore my passions.

Problem-Solving and Perseverance

I'm certain Liv's humorous observational breakdown of adults taking selfies rings true for many of you. Aside from being a kids-eye view of adults being awkward with tech, it also highlights our need to take more risks and explore the tech tools we use. Isn't it interesting the device we probably use the most, our phone, has simple, useful, and powerful features we are unaware of simply because we don't take the time to explore its capabilities?

Unlike adults, children almost always take the time to explore tech tools. One of my favorite watching-kids-explore-tech moments came from a visit to a kindergarten classroom where they were just beginning to create their own LivBit-style videos. One particularly loud student stood in front of his device and shouted, "Where's my forehead?" This question prompted others to look at their screens and momentarily consider the same thing. Quickly students began rotating their devices from horizontal plane to vertical, until foreheads were suitably visible in the frame.

This type of on-the-spot problem-solving is common when tech is used in the classroom and children are allowed the opportunity to explore, analyze, reflect, and revise. Children tend to persevere through a tech challenge, and even the most hesitant learner can learn from the risk-taking of others (Vygotsky, 1978). Encouraging a collaborative spirit and a press-pause-and-look-around strategy creates an authentic peer-to-peer problem-solving model.

Exploration Cycle

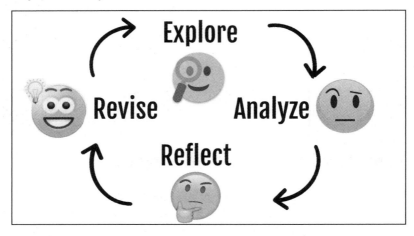

During the exploration cycle, the challenge for teachers is to hone their "kidwatching" skills—the practice of watching children with a "knowledgeable head" (Goodman & Owacki, 2002). Kidwatching grows the teacher's ability to categorize different types of learning engagement. Teachers note the kinds of strategies students use, along with the decisions they make when exploring ideas more deeply. Kidwatching allows teachers to consider the child's point of view in a learning situation. Understanding from this view can strengthen the types of differentiation that might happen in later inquiry. For example, when the student easily flips her device from a horizontal plane to a vertical one, the teacher can note this and see if the student problem-solves in a similar way during her next LivBit-style video. Teachers can consider the types of feedback they might offer the learner to strengthen problem-solving and perseverance. Remember the principles of feedback from Chapter Four:

- Is the feedback continuous?

- Is it co-constructed?

- Is it building the learner's confidence?

- Is it adding dimensions to the learner's thinking?

Liv's earlier analysis of adults being awkward with tech is exactly what effective anecdotal kidwatching notes would include, although in this instance it was "adult-watching." Perhaps there should be some consideration for empowering children to unpack adults' awkwardness with tech. This would provide an authentic opportunity for students to hone their mentor-tech skills, while also serving a true need to help adults become less awkward and more skillful with tech.

Maybe that's the next book Liv will write. I expect her observations would be spot on. I'm also certain my own occasional awkwardness would be fodder for Liv's content.

Reflection and Exploration

The use of technology in this kidwatching process creates numerous opportunities for reflection. Even a simple video collection can be reviewed with teacher notes, so what was seen in real time can be either confirmed or extended at the time of review. This use of technology to reflect gives teachers the opportunity to reconsider student decisions. In the process of reconsideration, teachers can frame their next teaching steps.

> Reconsider (verb): To think about all over again, especially when you want to change a decision; to change your mind.

Often, students are asked to create with tech tools but aren't asked to reflect on the process. When children can talk about their creations, reconsidering the decisions they made as learners, there's potential for incredible demonstration of student agency. Giving students time to reconsider the decisions they made in the learning process strengthens

Create and Share Tools

Name of App	Icon	Purpose
Pixie	Px	·record our thinking ·draw pictures ·take pictures ·share our work
Draw and Tell		·record ·draw and write
Kidblog	K	·post about your thinking ·see others thinking
Flipgrid	+	·recording videos ·share your thinking
Chatterkid		·make recordings to share thinking ·make mouth talk

opportunities for metacognition by encouraging the type of "thinking talk" that gives purpose to digital work (Vygotsky, 1978).

Allowing children to explore tools and apps isn't a new concept, but framing how the child might use the app is crucial. One simple but effective "appsploration" outcome can be an anchor chart of favorite classroom apps along with a description of the students' purposes for using them. The kindergarten "Create and Share Tools" anchor chart shown here is a perfect example that demonstrates co-creation with students. Teachers fill in the app name, followed by the icon, so students can easily identify the app when they are on their device. Finally, students describe the purpose for using the app.

Once the student has gained confidence creating in the apps, she can begin to interact more widely beyond teacher and classroom. Children's creations can often be shared with families with a simple click and, in some instances, can be shared even more globally, offering students the chance to interact and learn from a more diverse network.

> Kids love to know what apps are their teachers' favorites! Share with your students the types of apps you use, and let them know how they help you in your everyday life.

The Power of Global Connectedness

Liv has developed a global network of teachers who care, encourage, and inspire her to grow as a learner. She loves to hashtag these teachers by their location, for example: #MyTaiwanTeacher, #MyCanadaTeacher, and even #MyAlaskaTeacher. Liv has shared in previous chapters how she envisions her work being "for the world," so this system of hashtagging by location helps her track how fast her global network is growing. She even sets goals around her global connections and wants to have a teacher on every continent, as well as in every state in the United States.

One of the best "it's a small world" moments from Liv's hashtag tracking system came when her Taiwan and Malaysia teachers ended up in New York City at the same time for teacher professional development. Each teacher recognized the other and immediately wanted to connect back to Liv sharing the incredible serendipitous meet-up. Her teachers took a photo holding a phone picture in between them. This gesture symbolizes the power of Liv's network; without the connection to Liv's work, these teachers wouldn't have known one another. That's how powerful connectedness can be. It can inspire Liv's global teachers to find each other in a huge city and proudly share the meet-up with her.

MY GLOBAL NETWORK

#MyTaiwanTeacher

#MyMalaysiaTeacher

ME!!!!

Liv sees social media as a learning landscape; the platforms provide depth and richness to her learning life. It's true she's been a connected learner long enough that we can now do "six degrees of separation to Liv." She often receives messages about followers making it a point to show they've met each other just to surprise Liv. Her Taiwan and Malaysia teachers started this trend, and many others quickly followed suit.

This example illustrates how digital spaces are always personal—the potential for helping students navigate with an ethic-of-care mindset is always possible. For Liv, the work her global teachers share online is just as powerful as if she was sitting in their classrooms creating and learning alongside their students. This learning inspires her to think more deeply about her own work and generate new content to share on her platforms.

Liv has learned how to explore different apps from watching and analyzing the posts her global teachers have made. Her keen interest in understanding which apps are the most useful and fun for students to use motivates her to teach her followers how to use these apps to promote their work. This collaboration allows Liv to consider several factors in this creation process:

> *Appiness* is the feeling kids have when they find an app that helps them create and share their story with the world. Please help kids find their appiness.

- Does the app have more than one way for students to show their thinking?

- Are there options for sharing within the app?

- How easily can a student navigate within the app itself without a lot of pre-teaching?

Much of what Liv creates comes from this kind of exploration. For example, recently Liv posted about a book and received many comments from children and teachers expressing their own thoughts on it. Liv loved that she had inspired a global conversation about a book, and she knew there must be a better way to organize comments. It prompted her to create an online book club and find an app that would make comments accessible and easier to share. Her first book choice, *A Wrinkle in Time* (2007) by Madeleine L'Engle, was perfectly timed just before the movie debuted. Students who participated in Liv's book club generated an incredible buzz around the novel, proving to Liv how powerful talking about books can be when tech tools are used to magnify the conversation. In just two days, Liv's book club went international; children all over the world logged on and shared incredibly astute observations and thoughts on the plot, characters, and author's craft. This experience bolstered Liv's global reading purpose even further and made her more determined to explore apps and platforms for the purpose of encouraging global book experiences for children and teachers.

This exploration of global book conversations also helped Liv consider more deeply how a reader's perspective is influenced by cultural experiences. This isn't something Liv would have necessarily noticed or understood without explicit teacher instruction, but Liv's online work helped her identify cultural nuances in book interpretations from the comments left by other children. She began asking questions on the comment thread, initiating back and forth conversations with book club participants. Before she knew it, Liv began questioning her own reading lens and entered into text interpretation at a much deeper level.

During her digital book club work, Liv was surprised that children often chose to show their thinking in writing, even though the Padlet app she used enabled them to show their thinking in multiple modalities—writing, video creation, drawing, voice thread, or photographs. Liv wondered if this was a result of children not having enough experiences creating with tech tools in novel ways, so defaulting to the writing option was an easier way to engage in the task. With each new book club (check them out by scanning the QR codes), Liv made improvements to the way she structured it on the app. She also made sure she demonstrated examples of each modality, so children could see an example created to show thinking about the text.

A Wrinkle in Time

The Miraculous Journey of Edward Tulane

Exploration Is Continuous

As you can see, the beauty of digital exploration is that there is no endpoint. Not only does it yield a never-ending network of new peers and mentors, but also infinite opportunities for creative growth. After all, isn't that what exploration is all about—perpetual questioning, experimentation, and growth? Much of Liv's growth has come from being a mentor. Perhaps those experiences allow her to see most concretely the continuous nature and growing impact of her own digital exploration. And where better to see this than in her younger sister, Charlotte.

Liv made her first LivBit when she was eight years old, so Charlotte was just three years old when she began learning from Liv's creations. As you can imagine, Charlotte admires her sister's work, and Liv provided incredible modeling for her. Early on, Charlotte was able to thoughtfully talk about what her "project for the world" might be. On the one hand, she wanted to be just like her sister, but on the other, she wanted to create her own story.

Using the video feature on the iPad was something Charlotte could manage on her own, and as soon as she learned what the symbol for upload was, she could do that on her own too. Most of her videos went into a storage app, where she could share them with a few selected friends who very kindly commented and helped Charlotte grow her own story. At first, she mimicked Liv's style by talking about books and even using her catchphrase; then, slowly, glimpses of her own style began to emerge. For example, Charlotte masterfully spoke to her audience almost in stylized-soliloquy—leaning right into the camera and speaking eye-to-eye with her audience: "I like earthworms . . . can you too . . . (dramatic pause) . . . please!" Her videos were intuitively persuasive, and she cleverly crafted messages that included repetition that was immediately entertaining to her audience: "Earthworms eat and eat and eat and poop, and poop, and poop, every, every single day!" Charlotte's initial exploration of Liv's style allowed her to have a solid basis to delve into her own video creation later on.

Charlotte's exploration of Liv's style also gave Liv much to consider when working with students during school visits. As part of her LivBit work, Liv spends time as a visiting innovator in school communities around the world. These onsite visits provide incredible opportunities for Liv to lift the level of creation with students, while also allowing Liv to hone her skills as a mentor tech. Liv learns so much from these visits, including how children interpret her message while also considering their own. It's as if her work with Charlotte is the micro-version of prep, while the school visits are the macro.

Before Liv visited their school in Upper Arlington, Ohio, Kasey Althouse and her first graders made a deep dive into Liv's videos in preparation. First, they analyzed Liv's style, much like Asavavatana's students

Samson's Plan

1. **Introduce yourself.**
   "Hello! My name is _Samson li_."

2. **Ask a question to hook your audience.**
   Choose one:
   "Do you have a passion? I do!"
   "Have you ever thought about sharing your passion with the world? I have!"
   Your own idea: _____

3. **Share your message in a catchy way.**
   My passion is _writting_
   Here are some reasons why I love _whritting_
   1. I like whitting becose it will help me be an ather.
   2. becuse it is fun—it is fun to write becuse I get to write anything I want.

4. **End with a catch phrase.** just keep writting just keep Writting!!!!!!!

did in Taiwan and Charlotte did with Liv's videos. Then Althouse's first graders began brainstorming ideas for their own videos centered on their passions. In order to scaffold their video creation, Althouse provided a planning sheet (see Appendix A) for her students. This planning sheet allowed students to use Liv's framework, but their own ideas, so they could creatively craft their own Bits.

The simplistic framework of Liv's videos—greeting, question, message, and catchphrase ending—makes for easy replication by students who want to create their own LivBit-style videos but aren't sure where to begin. When children mimic Liv's style, just as Charlotte did, it gives them time to consider how to create a video with message, without the pressure of stylistic decisions. In time, as students develop their confidence within the LivBit framework, they typically explore more personal stylistic twists. Children find all of this exploration of craft and creation contagious. They seek out more and more examples of creators online, and they consider more complex style options for their videos. Once you engage students in this creation process, they begin to demonstrate an awareness of their identity and have a deeper sense of agency in their learning.

A year into her LivBit work, Liv added blogging as another piece of content. Initially, she intended to simply explore and discuss her own thinking—what she wondered, was trying to understand, or hoped for the world. At the beginning of her blogging journey, Liv was convinced no one ever read her posts. But, slowly over time, more and more teachers began reaching out, sharing with Liv how influential her words were for their students. Liv gained confidence in herself as a blogger and began taking on blogging projects beyond her own blog.

Just like with Liv's videos, many teachers have deconstructed Liv's blog posts to provide examples for their student bloggers. Liv's style in her blog posts mirrors the style she uses in her videos:

1. Start with a question to hook the audience.

2. Make sense of a big idea in a way that engages the audience.

3. End with a synthesis of your blog post's message and your catchphrase.

She also uses hashtags as titles as a way to provide a hint to her readers about the overall message of the post.

What's remarkable about Liv's blogging style is the way she's able to craft an authentic voice on issues or experiences she's had. Liv always shares how much she loves to talk, and it's possible the work she's done exploring the power of talk through her video creations has strengthened her writing skills. She writes exactly how she speaks, and this makes her writing accessible to her audience. Recently, she confessed to a friend, "I don't even really know what voice is, I just know I have it in my writing."

Diverse Spaces and Tools Invite Innovation

Whether it's blogging or book clubs, Liv's creation occurs in a variety of settings using many different tech tools depending on the task. Having diverse spaces, times, tech tools invites innovation.

Liv and I had the opportunity to visit the headquarters of a major gaming company in San Francisco, California. The office space is perched on top of the fiftieth floor of a beautiful building offering panoramic views of the city. We didn't find a bunch of cubicles where people worked in isolation; instead, we found comfy spots with many seating options, giant screens positioned for gaming practice, and a massive monitor filled with red dots representing all the places in the world people were currently playing the company's games. There were spaces flooded with bright light from the floor-to-ceiling windows and dimly lit spaces tucked into corners for when thinking required a different mood.

As Liv explored the space, including the incredible two-story slide that provided entertaining brain breaks for employees, I reflected on the push to diversify classroom spaces, offering more options for students to work collaboratively and comfortably. I thought about all the ways tech tools were used in this company and wondered if schools were giving children enough time to explore apps, tools, and collaborative digital spaces.

Think about time, space, and collaboration, and let your classroom evolve. Apps and platforms might come and go, but the thinking we teach students as they explore these digital spaces won't.

Louie DaCosta

@artfulouie: Innovative Designer

Exploring art with Louie through his snappy how-to drawing videos has become an instant favorite Saturday morning activity at my house. My sister, Charlotte, and I look forward to Louie's tutorial videos each weekend.

I feel super happy Louie is sharing his incredible love of art with the world. He said he was inspired by the work I did on LivBits: "When you shared your love of reading with the world, I realized any kid could share their passion with the world to make a difference." Louie explained how he had help from his mom getting his video routines: "My mom helped me ALL the way through thinking how I could share my love of art and we created #SatSketch as a way for others to make a difference sharing their art."

It's true kids can do important work for the world, and it's also true they need grown-ups who believe and encourage them. Louie's experiences posting his video tutorials have been successful because he's had a grown-up guiding and growing his understanding of different platforms.

So while Louie is sharing his art with the world, he is also learning important ideas about creating his story online. It's true, when you explore a passion, and you find ways to share that passion, you have the potential to influence how others feel about that topic. Louie hopes "the world realizes that there is an artist inside everyone."

And that's what making your mark in the digital world is all about—taking risks to share with an audience and encouraging others to never give up.

Louie's hashtag for the world: #BelieveInArt

Chapter Seven

Digital Future

> Have you ever thought about the sparks needed to ignite the future for kids and technology?

In this final chapter, we reverse roles: I lead the chapter, and Liv's words will take us into the future. It seems fitting to end with her ideas, because not only did she drive the content of this book, but also her work represents what's possible for students.

Liv's online work truly gives us a glimpse into the future. All children deserve the right to explore digital spaces as learners, deepen passions, and evolve and grow as individuals. LivBits is entirely a home project, so this final chapter is meant as a rallying cry for educators and parents to step up their digital commitments.

Shelley Harwayne, one of my favorite literacy authors, shared an idea in her book *Lasting Impressions* (1992) that's stayed with me my entire teaching career. Harwayne asserted:

> All our children need to believe they have something interesting to say. Literature plays a key role in helping children's voices take the floor. Literature triggers thoughts, unlocks memories, and helps

create the kind of community in which it's safe to tell our stories (p. 42).

At the beginning of my teaching life, I clutched Harwayne's words so tightly. They were a reminder for when I felt the inevitable pressures of curriculum, standards, or testing madness. Harwayne's words kept students and stories at the center of my teaching heart. I needed that center then, and I still need it now.

Harwayne's words were a harbinger for where I find myself today—profound sentiments I can use when thinking about the power of technology in children's lives.

As we look forward in this digital age, I offer this reboot of Harwayne's words: "All our children need to believe they have something interesting to say. Literature *and technology* play key roles in helping children's voices take the floor. Literature *and technology* trigger thoughts, unlock memories, and help create the kind of community in which it's safe to tell our stories."

Liv understands the power of her story. She uses that power to connect with incredible people who intensify her passions. The digital spaces she frequents will diversify as she grows, but the experiences she's having now are preparing her to continually look for opportunities to create meaning and grow her thinking.

Children need digital experiences connected to the ideas they care about because digital platforms are where their future resides. This entire book is about the meaning Liv has constructed from her LivBit content. Without the platforms to lift her story, Liv's work might sit in her backpack on our mudroom floor. Instead, her story is in the world, and that's because, as Liv always says, "it's for the world."

Technology in the hands of children sparks the change we need in the world. Let them tell their stories. Help them lift their stories. Believe their stories can change humanity.

> I learned another new word in the process of writing this book. As a friend was reading our chapters, she paused and said, "Liv, this book is like your salvo." I had no idea what that word meant, but Siri

Connection to the ISTE Standards

Educator Standard 2: Leader

Educators seek out opportunities for leadership to support student empowerment and success and to improve teaching and learning. Educators:

a. Shape, advance and accelerate a shared vision for empowered learning with technology by engaging with education stakeholders.

b. Advocate for equitable access to educational technology, digital content and learning opportunities to meet the diverse needs of all students.

c. Model for colleagues the identification, exploration, evaluation, curation and adoption of new digital resources and tools for learning.

Educator Standard 6: Facilitator

Educators facilitate learning with technology to support student achievement of the ISTE Standards for Students. Educators:

a. Foster a culture where students take ownership of their learning goals and outcomes in both independent and group settings.

b. Manage the use of technology and student learning strategies in digital platforms, virtual environments, hands-on makerspaces or in the field.

c. Create learning opportunities that challenge students to use a design process and computational thinking to innovate and solve problems.

d. Model and nurture creativity and creative expression to communicate ideas, knowledge or connections.

---

said it was "the first part of a speech or the first in a series of actions intended to get a particular result."

It's an incredibly powerful idea to imagine the ending of this book as really another beginning, like the first in a series of actions my mum

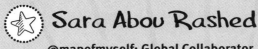

Sara Abou Rashed

@mapofmyself: Global Collaborator

When I thought about who my final Spotlight should be in this book, I knew the only person who could carry this book into the future with me was my friend Sara Abou Rashed.

As a Syrian immigrant to our country, Sara taught herself English by reading books. Now a college student, she's the creator of a one-woman show telling her immigrant story called "Map of Myself." She uses her social media platforms to share her show's message of tolerance, hope, and peace.

Sara is a role model for me in lots of ways, but most especially in how she uses words to share her message with the world. I had the opportunity to keynote with Sara at a conference and have never, ever been more riveted by how someone uses words than when I heard her speak.

Sara very beautifully defined how she sees the future:

> For me, the future is whatever comes *next*. The future is not just what's so far away in the distance; the future is tomorrow. The future is the next hour. The next minute. The next second. What's most exciting to think about is that the future cannot and will not happen without the now—we are already creating the future one second and one invention at a time.

Sara's vision of the future is so powerful. Her words are exactly how I see kids and technology. It's why every minute in your classrooms matter, and it's what makes access to technology so incredibly important.

Sara shared a bit of wisdom she holds onto from her high school social studies teacher, who told her that at every single moment, "we are the oldest and the wisest we have ever been, but the youngest and least knowledgeable we will ever be."

I hold onto Sara's wisdom and have learned so much from her. My favorite Sara reminder is that "we are complicated beings with complicated stories. Sometimes, our mission is to be the ones to stand out. To bring awareness. To remind people how very similar we all are on the inside—that the immigrant, and the black, and the Hispanic, and the genderqueer, and absolutely anyone—is a friend."

Sara's hashtags for the world:

- #mapofmyself
- #whatsyourmap

and I might be taking for the world. And it brings me back to why I love our title so much: *Spark Change.*

Sparks have the potential to start a fiery explosion of ideas. Your sparks can be your salvo.

This final chapter shares my biggest wishes for kids and tech. Imagine all the Spotlight stories as possibilities for your own work, and picture me in your mind, sitting in your class, wishing for more connected opportunities and encouraging your "Yes, I can!" feelings.

The students in your classrooms are the digital future. They need opportunities to understand how connecting can be powerful and safe. They need you to believe in the importance of technology in their lives. They need you to take risks in your own learning, so they can take risks with their own. They need you to be willing to let *them* lead the learning.

Think about the steps you can take to deepen your commitment to connected learning experiences—including the use of social media to create powerful learning networks for your students. Let authors, scientists, and visionaries mentor your students and help them see their future more clearly.

> Have class social media accounts and teach students how to post and comment. This is a powerful way for them to see how to show the world a story that matters!

I know all students need their teachers, but you have some students who might need you a bit more. Maybe they don't have access or support to use devices in creative ways. Maybe they haven't had opportunities to experience being the leader of their learning. Maybe they've been hurt by previous online experiences and haven't seen how technology can be used for digital good. Whatever the reason, kids need you to help them imagine what their future looks like, and that happens much more easily when they can explore tech tools that bring their dreams into sharper focus.

Hold your students in your heart as you read this final chapter, and remember all kids need your help connecting their digital dots. Imagine the students in your class and how you can take action to help them each connect to the world in meaningful ways. Catch the sparks and let them ignite your thinking and your classroom.

Spark Hope

Sparking hope starts with truly valuing student voice. You can do this by helping your students see how important their perspective is to you. It's not about telling the world you value student voice; it's about actually stepping up during critical times when a student may doubt her voice matters.

You can also be extra thoughtful about the feedback you give your students, and talk to your students about how to process feedback that's not so positive (see Chapter Four for my mum's excellent suggestions). Two of the most important things I've learned about giving and receiving feedback are to always question and to be aware of assumptions. Just like reading, when kids use tech tools, questioning is one of the most important strategies to promote understanding.

Having international followers giving me feedback on my content has helped me see the world in new ways. If I am honest, some of the places where my LivBit work has been shared or viewed are places I had never even heard of before. Lots of times, I have to find information about the little red dots that appear on my global blog tracker. I get excited by learning about different cultures and from talking with my global teachers. Now I consider how cultural influences impact the type of feedback those followers might offer me, and I ask more questions to understand exactly what they mean in a comment or a share.

Still, I know some people will make assumptions about me that aren't true. I know I have no control over that. But I do have control over how I handle the criticism and how I can use it to define my work even more deeply.

I've worked hard to create videos and other content that will inspire kids to read more books. I've also worked super hard to find ways to get books into the hands of kids. This means collaborating with book companies and sometimes authors, and it also means finding ways

Replying to @thelivbits @ChrisOCEARCH and 4 others

Im all for the kids but, I don't like her shirt, she doesn't have a clue what it means and it was mostly a political move by her mother...

to raise money to buy books for kids. It means never giving up on my dream to share books, because the truth is, it's not always easy to have big dreams when people criticize or doubt my intentions.

When I shared a LivBit I made with summer reading tips, I got an immediate comment about how lucky I was to have books to read over the summer. The comment mentioned kids who weren't as fortunate. The week before, I posted a personalized LivBit for a class in Ohio, and someone commented he didn't like the feminist message on my T-shirt and that it was probably just a "political move" by my mum.

I'm a thinker, so my brain goes back to these comments again and again. I think about how my posts are perceived by followers. I talk about it a lot with people, so I can get perspectives different from my own. I want to understand why followers assume I don't understand the needs of other kids or what the word feminist means. It bothers me, but it also lights sparks in me. This type of feedback makes me work harder to develop my LivBit message even more and to make my intentions clearer.

I'm for digital good. I want to be the kind of person who celebrates lots of diverse and important voices. I want people to see me as someone they can count on, and I want people to see me lifting other

Olivia Van Ledtje
@thelivbits

Dear Twitter, Please raise your hand if you think I show evidence of being a good reader, thinker, and speaker 👻 Today I sat through mindless testing for ELA. I promise it shows nothing about me as a learner. Too bad being a keynote speaker doesn't count for anything 🙄🙄

1:59 PM - 18 Apr 2018 from New Hampshire, USA

102 Retweets 406 Likes

people. Most importantly, I want to spark hope in other people to share their story with the world, but I need grown-ups to value my perspective.

Sometimes grown-ups don't give kids enough credit or think the things they say don't stick with us. Sometimes grown-ups take out an injustice they feel on other people, and when those people are kids, they expect us to just take it. They think we don't understand when their comments are cutting or snide, but it's during these times kids feel hopeless.

Instead, I use all of my content and my social media platforms to share my hope with the world. I know not all kids have the same opportunities. I spend a lot of time feeling worries for other kids. I wish kids everywhere had the same kinds of experiences with books that I do. I know this isn't always possible, but that's also one of the reasons I started LivBits. I think when kids hear messages from other kids, they listen more, and they get hopeful and inspired, too.

Sometimes I seek out feedback when I need a little hope, so I share my thinking directly with my audience by writing notes. I've found that when I write these kinds of notes, my audience gets hopeful too, and they leave me all kinds of feedback to consider. When people begin sharing hopeful thoughts, it's like so many heartbeeps going out to the world, and that's what sparking hope is all about, sharing more and more so that your hope sparks heartbeeps for the world.

My biggest hope is for all kids to have people who value their voices and lift their stories for the world. And the biggest heartbeeps I've had from my school-based work is with kids who create with hope in their hearts and a desire to make the world better.

Let's fill the world with heartbeeps and spark hope!

> Ask your students to write a letter to the world in the form of a tweet. Encourage them to share their hope for the world in 240 characters or less.

Spark Story

My LivBit story is about the power of being a connected learner. Many people in my digital networks have become people who, I know, will be in my life forever—digital connections that have turned into real friendships. I didn't have to wait until I was a grown-up to see the power of my passions; I'm learning my passions are important and can drive the learning I do in and out of school. They can help me understand and change the world.

One of the most important things I've learned from LivBits is how much learning can happen when you see the world as your class-room. I am so lucky that I have teachers in my life who are all over the world encouraging my stories! Being a connected learner means having opportunities to learn from kid activists, authors, scientists, ballerinas, and people I admire and wish to be like. It also means having the opportunity to visit schools and work with kids and teachers sharing my message #KidsCanTeachUs. It means being inspired by those people too!

I've also learned that my story matters. I am the child of stories. I read. I think. I talk. I share. I learn.

And here's the thing: We *all* have stories. You too! Share your story with your students. Kids can't learn from people they don't connect with, so sharing your story matters! And remember, sometimes those connections can start out digitally, and they're just as important.

It's important kids understand they create a story online. When they like or share something, they are offering feedback. Making comments is a powerful way of connecting to another person's story, so being aware of how those comments will be received is super important. Having a #Digital4Good mindset can draw people to your message. I've been asked loads of times to help other people get more followers. Honestly, it's not the number of followers that matters, it's about the power of your story. When you create a story that matters, people will be drawn to your light.

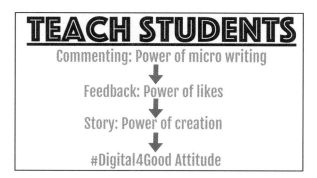

After reading this book, I hope you'll consider all the ways creating and sharing has helped me understand the world more and look for ways to make social media more accessible to kids in your school. Social media platforms can be places where kids can learn to love the world more, and I'm an example of that. I have found more people who encourage than discourage, more heartbeeps than heartache. Please commit to never underestimating the power of a kid's voice and the power of their story. When your students see their story as an important piece of their future, they will work to create a story that matters. Encourage kids to share their story and help them learn from the feedback they receive. Show them how their story can be the spark that influences other people's stories too. Believe every spark has the potential to make a difference.

 Want to be a changemaker? Here's how to start!

- Read a lot.
- Talk a lot.
- Share your thinking a lot.
- Ask questions a lot.
- Be for DIGITAL GOOD.

If you do all of those things, you can change the world!

Spark Action

There are lots of ways my LivBit work has helped me think bigger than my own community. When I receive messages from other kids about my work, I feel super motivated to create more and to help more. They spark me to take action!

Last Christmas, I received a ukulele, and I've spent the last year teaching myself how to play. It's been a lot of hard work, but I've loved learning a new instrument. I feel grateful I have another way to express myself, and another reason to connect and learn from other people who love books and music too.

I think it's important for kids to have lots of ways to show their thinking. Maybe for some kids it's by making videos, like I make. For others, it might be writing their thinking out in a story. Or it might be playing a tune on a ukulele!

Recently, I had the honor of visiting a school in Ohio for my LivBit work. This school is special to me for loads of reasons and especially because of their music and ukulele program, which is cherished by the students. Unfortunately, this school is 100% free breakfast and lunch for all students and lacks the funds to keep the ukuleles for an entire year. Kids at this school use the ukuleles for only a few months, then need to pass them on to the other schools in the district.

During my visit, this school gave me a gift. After my LivBit keynote, they surprised me by singing my favorite song, "This Is Me," from *The Greatest Showman*. I will never, ever forget the special feeling of having 500 voices singing those lyrics to me. I was so grateful to them for giving me such a gift. They inspired me to try to find a way to give back to them. They sparked in me an idea and a desire to take action: What if I could raise money to help this school get a set of 25 ukuleles for its music program—ukuleles they could keep and learn to play for the entire year?

I created an online campaign and began sharing it on all my plat-forms. I also set up a table at a local bookstore and drew holiday pictures for people. I knocked on my neighbors' doors and asked if they could help. I let my family and friends know I didn't want anything for Christmas except to get my ukuleles funded. I also reached out to the company who makes the ukes to ask if I could make a deal with them: If I raised enough money for 25 ukuleles, would they offer me free shipping? Not only did they answer yes, but they also threw in lots of freebies for the school, including bags to store the ukes and free online lessons for the kids.

None of this was easy, but I learned so much in the process of my ukulele project. First, I learned, it's tricky to ask people for money. Not everyone values the same things you value, so you have to be willing to hear lots of noes before you get a yes. I learned how important it is to share your passion clearly, so people can connect to your purpose. And I learned there are so many heartbeeps that come from thinking bigger than your own community.

This gift might seem like it's for one school, but it's really for the entire Ohio community where this school is located. By purchasing this school its own set of ukuleles, the other schools will have the existing ukuleles for longer. The students and their families will benefit, and I am certain the schools will perform for many people. In other words, my ukulele campaign helped me spark a small piece of musical joy in this community. One experience truly can spark action!

Recently, I received a poem from a second grader who lives in New York. His poem was part of a unit his teacher did about activists. I'm so grateful his teacher, Mrs. Daley, shared my LivBit message with her class, and even more grateful Austin was inspired enough to study my videos. He created a poem titled "One Girl" to show his understanding. Austin's poem perfectly captures what I hope people see in my work. What's even more special is how my work sparked Austin to take action with words. Kids are so incredible!

One Girl: Olivia Van Ledtje
By Austin, second grader

One Girl
as young as me
can teach teachers.
Loves reading,
loves sharks
fighting for
no bullying,
no boy's and girl's things.
Fighting for kids
because kids can teach us.
She impacted us by
making LivBits,

traveling to different schools,
gives speeches.
One girl
as young as me
can teach teachers
and she made a promise.
A promise that
she will always
do good things for the world,
and we can too.

You don't have to be a grown-up to care deeply about another person, or to have wishes bigger than the present moment. Kids can have those feelings too. Kids can understand the power of being there for each other and can encourage each other's dreams. Receiving Austin's poem proved to me how powerful it is when you create from your heart—people will notice! I don't think I'm unusual; I think most kids create from their hearts. That's why so many kids take time out of their day to draw a picture or write a note for a special person. Kids have hearts that are open to the world, and when we show them how much the world cares, they will be sparked to do more.

> Follow people who make you smile about the world. Share your happiness and celebrate other people's happiness, too.

I've never met a kid who doesn't have desires and wishes to do something good for the world. It's just each kid shows desire in different ways. So, if you're a grown-up reading this, and you're wishing for more heartbeeps, just find a kindergartener and ask them about something they love. I promise, you'll find heartbeeps by listening to them, and maybe those heartbeeps will create sparks in you to find ways to help kids have more tech opportunities.

Recently, I was a visiting innovator in a district in Ohio. While I was there, I saw a wall filled with tweets the students wrote to me about my work. All of the tweets gave me heartbeeps, but one in particular stood out from the rest because it assured me my work was needed online. I'm so grateful to the student who wrote this message. It's one I will carry with me forever.

> Check your emoji line-up, and if the happy emojis aren't to the left, send some out to friends so happy emojis are the first thing you see when you open your device.

People always ask me for advice about being online, and usually I feel like my best advice is right in my LivBit videos. But this time, I want to offer you Austin's words as a start: Make a promise and do good things for the world. When you see an injustice, speak up, but do it kindly and with words that help people see another perspective. Pay attention to other people's words and remember that words can light sparks, and those sparks can lead to action.

Make your mark on the world by sharing a hopeful story others can't help but notice. And remember, you're the best spark the world could ever ask for. Go out and make your mark. The world will be brighter because you did.

Let's spark change forever.

Lesson Ideas to Try

One of the many advantages of having Liv's work shared in many corners of the world is the incredible ways teachers and students create their own meaning and purpose from her message. Throughout this book, we have tried to offer many practical application examples from Liv, but we also wanted to offer more formal examples written in lesson plan format. It's our hope that as you read this book, you are able to imagine your own students and their passions being shared with a global audience, and that each of the avenues we have provided—practical and formal lesson plans—will be useful.

The lessons are aligned with the ISTE Standards for Students, and most provide extension activities that can be used across content areas. Although Liv's work is in the area of literacy, many teachers and students have shared examples of their own work representing creative use of tech tools and a plethora of ideas for content areas.

Breaking the News

Objective

Students will evaluate individual situations and create positive communication skills for each situation.

ISTE Standards Addressed

- Student Standard 2: Digital Citizen: a, b, c, and d
- Student Standard 6: Creative Communicator: a, b, c, and d

Materials

Whiteboard or LCD monitor

Steps

1. Make groups of 4–5 students each.
2. Post the following list of situations for students to see:
   - Late to work
   - Break up with boy/girlfriend
   - Family emergency
   - Canceling on someone
   - Birthday
   - Need a ride
   - Need help with something
   - Argument within a text
   - Argument with parent
   - Need help with school
   - Promposal announcement
   - Not doing well in class
3. Ask: How would they handle each possible situation, and why? Text? Call? Face-to-face? Post on social?

Discussion Questions

- Did everyone handle all the situations the same?
- Did anyone change their mind on how they handled a situation after hearing someone else's viewpoint?
- Can you handle every situation exactly the same? Why, or why not?
- If you choose to post something on social media, is there ever a time you should call or text someone before you post about it? When?
- When you post content online, do you expect everyone to know about it?

Discussion Notes

- Discuss the illusion "just because you post about it, it doesn't mean everyone saw it."
- People post about death before family even knows about it.

#IDIDHELP Challenge

In a text, in an email, or on a 3×5 card, create sentence starters to start these conversations:

- I would like to ...
- Can I please explain ...
- I understand how you feel ...

Credit: Activity courtesy of @ICANHELP

 **Mirror Illusion**

Objective

Students will critique the effects of being a positive role model on and off social media.

ISTE Standards Addressed

- Student Standard 2: Digital Citizen: a, b, c, and d
- Student Standard 6: Creative Communicator: a, b, c, and d

Materials

Internet access to online video

Steps

1. Figure out who is Partner A and Partner B.
2. Have Partner B imitate A's movements.
3. Switch, and allow A to imitate B's movements.
4. Watch the *Uncap the Possibilities* episode: "Aaron Judge's Mission to Delete Negativity from the Internet" on YouTube (3:15 minutes).

Aaron Judge's Mission

Discussion Questions

- Did your partner make it easy for you, or was it hard to follow their lead?
- Has anyone ever imitated something you were doing? If so, what?
- Have you seen any fake sites or impersonation sites on social media? How do you or would you handle them?
- Who do you look up to as a role model? Who do you think looks up to you?

- Who in your family follows you on social media? In life?
- Who is the oldest person who follows you or who you would let follow you?
- Who is the youngest person who follows you or who you would let follow you?
- Is there someone you don't or wouldn't let follow you? Why?
- Do you feel like you are a good role model online? Offline?

Discussion Notes

- Go over how to report fake or hate accounts.
- There are real people who look at the reports, and it only takes one person to report something. If multiple people report a page or post, however, it will get taken down faster.
- Tag @ICANHELP or DM a screenshot to @ICANHELP for help as well.

Credit: *Activity courtesy of @ICANHELP*

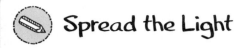

Spread the Light

Objective

This instructional experience is designed to encourage communication and openness about online bullying experiences as well as strategies to cope. Students will reflect on their digital interactions and how to both ask for and give support.

> **Today I am** thinking about how I interact with people digitally,
> **So I can** be myself in public and private spaces.
> **I'll know I've got it when** I can tell when I need to ask for or give help.

ISTE Standards Addressed

- Student Standard 2: Digital Citizen: a, b, c, and d
- Student Standard 6: Creative Communicator: a, b, c, and d

Materials

Whiteboard or LCD monitor

Steps

1. Share the following comment with students:

> Comment
> Dear Liv,
>
> You are the worst. I know it's great when children share messages, but not when they're stuck up and operating from a website their mom obviously edits. Your voice is also REALLY annoying. There. I said it. Ok. Anyways, those words are not yours. Also, just in case you're terrible at math, becoming 11 and going into the sixth grade is not the threshold to adult life. It's just middle school. Get a grip, snooty, annoying Liv!!

2. Have students turn and talk about discussion questions provided below.
3. Show students how to spread the light with a positive tweet back to Liv.

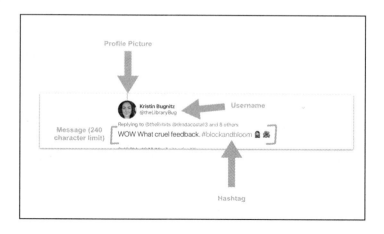

Discussion Questions

- Have you seen this happen online?
- How would you react?
- What advice would you give Liv?

Writing Extension

Have students work in pairs creating their own positive tweet back to Liv.

Credit: *Activity courtesy of Kristin Bugnitz @theLibraryBug*

3D Book Review

Objective

Students will create a 3D book review using a MERGE Cube. It will be about a book of their choosing and will look like the example found by following the QR code:

MERGE Cube Hacks

ISTE Standards Addressed

- Student Standard 2: Digital Citizen: a, b, c, and d
- Student Standard 3: Knowledge Constructor: a, b, c, d
- Student Standard 6: Creative Communicator: a, b, c, and d

Materials

- Tablet with CoSpaces Edu app (Pro version) and MERGE Cube add-on
- CoSpaces Edu teacher account (to provide student access)
- MERGE Cubes
- Google Slides (for book review templates)

Steps

1. Introduce the 3D book review format.
2. Create the book review templates in Google Slides. Pages include: TAG (title, author, genre), Characters, Setting, Rating, Summary, and Download as JPG.
3. Log in to CoSpaces Edu, import book review pages, and place them on the MERGE cube.
4. Use a tablet with the CoSpaces Edu app to view a MERGE Cube to see the book review in 3D!

Discussion Questions

- Why should your audience love this book?
- Why are you excited about this book?
- How does your MERGE Cube review highlight the power of the story?

Challenge

What else can you create using a MERGE Cube and CoSpaces Edu?

Credit: *Activity courtesy of @MerkleJill (adapted from Mary Howard)*

Kids Can Teach Us: Te'Lario Watkins

Objective

Help kids share their passions with the world using technology.

ISTE Standards Addressed

- Student Standard 2: Digital Citizen: a, b, c, and d
- Student Standard 3: Knowledge Constructor: a, b, c, d
- Student Standard 7: Global Collaborator; a, b, c, d

Materials

LCD monitor

Steps

Tiger Mushroom Farms

1. Introduce Tiger Mushroom Farms.
2. Share the video with your students: Columbus Neighborhoods: Tiger Mushroom Farms.
3. Use the resources and questions below for discussion.

8-Year-Old Mushroom Mogul

10-Year-Old Grows Business

10-Year-Old Shares Love

Discussion Questions

- Who is Te'Lario?
- How did Te'Lario follow his passions?
- What are you passionate about?
- How can you share your passion?

Activity Extension

1. Find something you love to do.
2. Do some research. (Ask for help if you need it.)
3. Come up with an idea of something awesome you could do around your passion that would raise awareness or do something good for the world.
4. Pair up and interview a partner about their idea.

Challenge

1. Create a business to share your passion.
2. Create a LivBit-style selfie video to share your business idea.
3. Include the four features of a selfie video (based on Liv's style guidelines).

LivBit Style

1. Introduce yourself

2. Ask a question to hook your audience

3. Share your message in a catchy way

4. End with a catch phrase

LivBit-Style Guidelines

4. Film your video in Flipgrid.

Credit: *Activity courtesy of Kristin Bugnitz @theLibraryBug*

The #SatSketch Process

Objective

Students will create a video tutorial about a personal passion for a global audience similar to Louie DaCosta's #SatSketch videos.

ISTE Standards Addressed

- Student Standard 2: Digital Citizen: a, b, c, and d
- Student Standard 6: Creative Communicator: a, b, c, and d

Materials

- iPhone/iPad with camera
- iMovie
- Any platform to publish edited videos: YouTube, Vimeo, Flipgrid, Seesaw (optional)
- Drawing materials
- Mentor tech: Artfulouie Channel

Artfulouie Channel

Steps

1. Set up student cameras using book stack and two pencils (see photo). The two pencils act as a "multipurpose" stand to prop the device used to record in selfie and bird's eye modes.

2. Have students record their tutorials in the following sections:
   a. Introduction. Place the camera in selfie mode to greet the audience and set purpose for the video.

b. Fact share. Share what exactly is going to be done and add a researched fact.

c. Demonstrate. Place the camera into bird's eye view mode to record the process of creating the drawing (or whatever it is you want to show).

d. Closing. Display the finished product and encourage your audience to participate and share their work via a shared hashtag. A special shout-out can be included prior to stating the personalized closing tagline.

3. Create a movie in iMovie and add recorded clips in sequence. Add any pictures before and after the video clips from the camera roll.

4. Edit the movie. Some fine-tuning suggestions include:

a. Make the voice louder when speaking, and mute the sound during the demonstration video clip if speaking is unnecessary.

b. Add a layer of music from the iMovie library.

c. Increase the speed of the demo video.

5. Upload the students' movies to the sharing platform of your preference.

Discussion Questions

- What is something you are passionate about and want to show others how to do?
- How does sharing your passion help the world?
- How does sharing your passion change the world?

Discussion Notes

- Because Louie had a difficult time holding on to all that he wanted to say in one long recording, he records his #SatSketch in parts.
- Louie makes a schedule and plans his videos ahead of time.

- Brevity is key. It is important for students to study various tutorials and consider which tutorials are more effective: short or lengthy ones. Why?

Writing Extension

- Students write a predictable introduction for their tutorial that includes a purpose.
- Students write a succinct tagline to close out their tutorial that represents their passion and best self.
- Students can research their passion.

Challenge

Students can use social media to connect with experts about their passion. For example, Louie follows many artists and illustrators to get more ideas for his #SatSketch videos, just like Liv follows shark experts to get more information for her projects.

Credit: *Activity courtesy of Diana DaCosta @dmdacosta13*

Show and Tell

Objective

Students will understand that effective teaching videos both show and tell instructions clearly.

ISTE Standards Addressed

- Student Standard 1: Empowered Learner: c
- Student Standard 2: Digital Citizen: a
- Student Standard 6: Creative Communicator: a, b, c, and d

Materials

- iPhone/iPad with camera
- Ability to project the iPhone/iPad onto a larger screen (optional)
- Seesaw or other video recording app with a pause function
- Any platform to publish edited videos: YouTube, Vimeo, Flipgrid, Seesaw (optional)
- Playing cards or materials used in a math game

Steps

1. Set up the selfie recording station. Have students sit or kneel with their backs against a wall and use a chair with a back to place the recording device on (see photo). Other parts of the chair can be used to lay out props and materials. Cue cards can even be taped above the device on the back of the chair if needed.

2. Make connections. Discuss how today people often learn how to do things by watching videos. Using math games that have been played frequently in class, explain that the students are now experts and will be creating videos that teach others how to play these games. *Possible Teaching Point: "Today you will learn that strong teaching videos both show and tell the viewer the instructions…"*

3. With selfie station set up, demonstrate how to position your body in front of the camera. If possible, project the iPad onto a larger screen so you can demonstrate things like noticing where your face is positioned on the screen and how to show props clearly to the camera. Introduce the strategy Pause-Practice-Present by explaining that creating videos using the pause function can help us plan our thinking in smaller chunks. Once again demonstrate how this could go.

4. Encourage active engagement: As you demonstrate pausing, practicing, and presenting the steps to a math game, take this as an opportunity to do some interactive modeling. Ask students to watch how you plan what you will say, record, pause, then repeat. This may also be a good opportunity to demonstrate how to use or show props such as playing

cards. After this, have the students turn and talk, sharing one thing they noticed you do. Ask for some students to share back with the rest of the class and highlight anything else that you feel they may have missed.

5. Link it all together: Tell the students that today they are going to use the Pause-Practice-Present routine to share

their expertise as they show and tell how to play a math game in their videos.

6. In small groups or individually, have students spread out around the room with their selfie recording stations. If needed, students first can plan out what they would like to say on index cards so that the video is set up in chunks. Providing an outline for planning can be helpful as well. Here is a possible outline for students to plan their videos:

   a. Introduction. Share the purpose of the video.
   b. Preparation. Share what the audience may need to prepare to play the game.
   c. Key steps. How is the game played? What do you need to tell the audience, and what do you need to show the audience to ensure they understand what to do?
   d. State the goal. What is the goal of this game? How do you know if you've won?
   e. Wrap it up. How can you wrap up the video in a catchy way?

7. Once the videos are done, publish them to be shared with classmates, family members, and a wider global audience, if possible. Ask family members to watch the videos at home to learn the game and play it at home as well. Students can then receive direct feedback from their family members to see how clearly the game was taught and if they understood how to play it.

Discussion Questions

- What are the most important things you need to know in order to play this math game?
- What is the goal of the game? How do you win, or how does the game finish?
- What are you learning when you are playing this game?
- When should you simply explain something (tell), and when is it important to also demonstrate something (show)?

Discussion Notes

- Some students may want to write out a plan using the outline in the mini-lesson (see step 6) before they start recording, whereas others may be able to simply use the outline to begin recording without writing it out first.
- Working in partnerships or small groups can help during the practice stage of the routine. Students can rehearse what they want to say using their peers as a practice audience that can give them impromptu feedback before recording.

Activity Extension

- Students can comment on each other's videos providing a round of feedback. They can look for areas of improvement such as volume of speech, clarity of instructions, and so on. They can use this feedback to improve their videos in a final cut.
- Share videos with another class in the same school or at another school. Have those students follow the steps in the videos to play the game and send back videos of them playing, so your class can see if the other students were able to learn the game effectively. This could potentially also be used as feedback for future video creation.

Studen Video of Lesson

Credit: *Activity courtesy of Pana Asavavatana @PanaAsavavatana*

Appendix A

LivBit Planning Sheet

1. Introduce yourself.

"Hello! My name is _____."

2. Ask a question to hook your audience.

Choose one:

- "Do you have a passion? I do!"
- "Have you ever thought about sharing your passion with the world? I have!"

Your own idea: _____

_____

_____

_____

_____

_____

_____

3. Share your message in a catchy way.

My passion is _____

_____ .

Here are some reasons why I love _____

-    _____

-    _____

4. End with a catchphrase.

Appendix B

ISTE Standards for Students

The ISTE Standards for Students emphasize the skills and qualities we want for students, enabling them to engage and thrive in a connected, digital world. The standards are designed for use by educators across the curriculum, with every age student, with a goal of cultivating these skills throughout a student's academic career. Both students and teachers will be responsible for achieving foundational technology skills to fully apply the standards. The reward, however, will be educators who skillfully mentor and inspire students to amplify learning with technology and challenge them to be agents of their own learning.

1. Empowered Learner

Students leverage technology to take an active role in choosing, achieving and demonstrating competency in their learning goals, informed by the learning sciences. Students:

    a.   articulate and set personal learning goals, develop strategies leveraging technology to achieve them and reflect on the learning process itself to improve learning outcomes.

    b.   build networks and customize their learning environments in ways that support the learning process.

c. use technology to seek feedback that informs and improves their practice and to demonstrate their learning in a variety of ways.

d. understand the fundamental concepts of technology operations, demonstrate the ability to choose, use and troubleshoot current technologies and are able to transfer their knowledge to explore emerging technologies.

2. Digital Citizen

Students recognize the rights, responsibilities and opportunities of living, learning and working in an interconnected digital world, and they act and model in ways that are safe, legal and ethical. Students:

a. cultivate and manage their digital identity and reputation and are aware of the permanence of their actions in the digital world.

b. engage in positive, safe, legal and ethical behavior when using technology, including social interactions online or when using networked devices.

c. demonstrate an understanding of and respect for the rights and obligations of using and sharing intellectual property.

d. manage their personal data to maintain digital privacy and security and are aware of data-collection technology used to track their navigation online.

3. Knowledge Constructor

Students critically curate a variety of resources using digital tools to construct knowledge, produce creative artifacts and make meaningful learning experiences for themselves and others. Students:

a. plan and employ effective research strategies to locate information and other resources for their intellectual or creative pursuits.

b. evaluate the accuracy, perspective, credibility and relevance of information, media, data or other resources.

c. curate information from digital resources using a variety of tools and methods to create collections of artifacts that demonstrate meaningful connections or conclusions.

d. build knowledge by actively exploring real-world issues and problems, developing ideas and theories and pursuing answers and solutions.

4. Innovative Designer

Students use a variety of technologies within a design process to identify and solve problems by creating new, useful or imaginative solutions. Students:

a. know and use a deliberate design process for generating ideas, testing theories, creating innovative artifacts or solving authentic problems.

b. select and use digital tools to plan and manage a design process that considers design constraints and calculated risks.

c. develop, test and refine prototypes as part of a cyclical design process.

d. exhibit a tolerance for ambiguity, perseverance and the capacity to work with open-ended problems.

5. Computational Thinker

Students develop and employ strategies for understanding and solving problems in ways that leverage the power of technological methods to develop and test solutions. Students:

a. formulate problem definitions suited for technology-assisted methods such as data analysis, abstract models and algorithmic thinking in exploring and finding solutions.

b. collect data or identify relevant data sets, use digital tools to analyze them, and represent data in various ways to facilitate problem-solving and decision-making.

c. break problems into component parts, extract key information, and develop descriptive models to understand complex systems or facilitate problem-solving.

d. understand how automation works and use algorithmic thinking to develop a sequence of steps to create and test automated solutions.

6. Creative Communicator

Students communicate clearly and express themselves creatively for a variety of purposes using the platforms, tools, styles, formats and digital media appropriate to their goals. Students:

a. choose the appropriate platforms and tools for meeting the desired objectives of their creation or communication.

b. create original works or responsibly repurpose or remix digital resources into new creations.

c. communicate complex ideas clearly and effectively by creating or using a variety of digital objects such as visualizations, models or simulations.

d. publish or present content that customizes the message and medium for their intended audiences.

7. Global Collaborator

Students use digital tools to broaden their perspectives and enrich their learning by collaborating with others and working effectively in teams locally and globally. Students:

a. use digital tools to connect with learners from a variety of backgrounds and cultures, engaging with them in ways that broaden mutual understanding and learning.

b. use collaborative technologies to work with others, including peers, experts or community members, to examine issues and problems from multiple viewpoints.

c. contribute constructively to project teams, assuming various roles and responsibilities to work effectively toward a common goal.

d. explore local and global issues and use collaborative technologies to work with others to investigate solutions.

References

Asavatatana, P. (2019). Ms. Pana Says. Retrieved August 1, 2019, from www.mspanasays.com

Collier, A. (2018). Net Family News. Retrieved August 1, 2019, from www.netfamilynews.org

Csikszentmihalyi, M. (1975). *Beyond boredom and anxiety: Experiencing flow in work and play*. San Francisco, CA: Jossey-Bass.

Csikszentmihalyi, M. (1990). *Flow: The psychology of optimal experience*. New York, NY: Harper & Row.

Csikszentmihalyi, M. (1996). *Creativity: Flow and the psychology of discovery and invention*. New York, NY: Harper Perennial.

Csikszentmihalyi, M. (1998). *Finding flow: The psychology of engagement with everyday life*. New York, NY: Basic Books.

Csikszentmihalyi, M. (2002). *Flow: The classic work on how to achieve happiness*. London: Rider.

Csikszentmihalyi, M. & Csikszentmihalyi, I. S. (Eds.). (1988). *Optimal experience: Psychological studies of flow in consciousness*. Cambridge, UK: Cambridge University Press.

Deci, E. L., & Ryan, R. M. (1985). *Intrinsic motivation and self-determination in human behavior*. New York, NY: Plenum.

Deci, E. L., & Ryan, R. M. (2000). Self-determination theory and the facilitation of intrinsic motivation, social development, and well-being. *American Psychologist, 55*(1), 68.

Deci, E. L., & Ryan, R. M. (2000). The "what" and "why" of goal pursuits: Human needs and the self-determination of behavior. *Psychological Inquiry, 11*, 227–268.

Deci, E. L., & Ryan, R. M. (2002). *Handbook of self-determination research*. Rochester, NY: University of Rochester Press.

Deci, E. L., & Ryan, R. M. (2008). Self-determination theory: A macrotheory of human motivation, development, and health. *Canadian Psychology/Psychologie Canadienne, 49*, 182–185.

Dewey, J. (1916). *Democracy and education.* New York, NY: The Free Press.

Dorn, L., & Soffos, C. (2005). *Teaching for deep comprehension: A reading workshop approach.* Portland, ME: Stenhouse.

Fleischman, Paul. (1988). *Joyful noise: Poems for two voices.* HarperCollins, Australia.

Fountas, I., & Pinnell, G. S., (2007). The continuum of literacy learning, grades K–8: Behaviors and understandings to notice, teach, and support. Portsmouth, NH: Heinemann.

Frank, Anne. (1993). *Anne Frank: The diary of a young girl.* New York, NY: Bantam.

Gardner, H., Csikszentmihalyi, M., & Damon, W. (2002). *Good business: Leadership, flow, and the making of meaning.* New York, NY: Basic Books.

Goodman, Y. M., & Owacki, G. (2002). *Kidwatching: Documenting children's literacy development.* Portsmouth, NH: Heinemann.

Harwayne, S. (1992). *Lasting impressions: Weaving literature into the writing workshop.* Portsmouth, NH: Heinemann.

Ito, M., Baumer, S., Bittani, M., boyd, d., Cody, R., Herr-Stephenson, B., . . . Tripp, L. (2010). *Hanging out, messing around, and geeking out: Kids living and learning with new media.* Cambridge, MA: MIT Press.

Lang, Heather. (2016). *Swimming with sharks: The daring discoveries of Eugenie Clark.* Chicago, IL: INDPB.

L'Engle, Madeleine. (2007). *A wrinkle in time.* New York, NY: Square Fish.

Mattson, K. [DrKMattson]. (2016, November 2). @SocialAssurity @MatthewSoeth @jasonohler @MattMurrie YES!! That girl gets social justice & is having a voice! [Tweet]. Retrieved August 1, 2019, from www.twitter.com/search?l=&q=social%20OR%20justice%20from%3ADrKMattson%20to%3Anancywtech%20%40thelivbits&src=typd

Mattson, K. (2017). *Digital citizenship in action: Empowering students in online communities.* Portland, OR: ISTE.

McGovern, Ann. (1978). *Shark Lady: True adventures of Eugenie Clark.* New York, NY: Scholastic Inc.

Merkle, J. (2019). The Page Turning Librarian. Retrieved August 1, 2019, from www.thepageturninglibrarian.blogspot.com

Newman, C. (2018). Precious Presence. Retrieved August 1, 2019, from www.preciouspresenceteaching.blogspot.com

Nichols, M. (2006). *Comprehension through conversation: The power of purposeful talk in the reading workshop.* Portsmouth, NH: Heinemann.

Noddings, N. (1984). *Caring: A feminine approach to ethics and moral education.* Berkeley, CA: University of California Press.

November, A. (2012). *Who owns the learning: Preparing kids for success in the digital age.* Bloomington, IN: Solution Tree Press.

Perkins, D. N., & Salomon, G. (1992). Transfer of learning. In *International Encyclopedia of Education, 2nd Edition, 11,* 6452–57. Oxford, UK: Pergamon Press.

Pink, D. H. (2009). *Drive: The surprising truth about what motivates us.* New York, NY: Riverhead Books.

Poynton, C. (2018, June 18). Children's rights online: An interview with UNICEF's Patrick Geary. *Article One.* Retrieved August 1, 2019, from www.articleoneadvisors.com/insights/2018/6/15/childrens-rights-online

Ribble, M. (2015). *Digital citizenship in schools: Nine elements all students should know.* Portland, OR: ISTE.

Royal, T. A. C. (2007, September 24). Papatūānuku—the land—tūrangawaewae—a place to stand. *Te Ara—The Encyclopedia of New Zealand.* Retrieved August 1, 2019, from www.TeAra.govt.nz/en/papatuanuku-the-land/page-5

United Nations Children's Fund (UNICEF) and the Guardian. (May 2016). Children's rights and the internet: From guidelines to practice. Retrieved August 1, 2019, from www.unicef.org/csr/files/Childrens_Rights_and_the_Internet_Guidelines_to_Practice_Guardian_Sustainble_Business_English.pdf

University of Oxford. (2017, December 14). Children's screen-time guidelines too restrictive, according to new research. Retrieved August 1, 2019, from www.ox.ac.uk/news/2017-12-14-children's-screen-time-guidelines-too-restrictive-according-new-research#

Vygotsky, L. S. (1978). *Mind in society.* Cambridge, MA: Harvard University Press.

Index

Global Collaborator Student Standard, 122–123, 136–137. *See also* collaboration

global collaborators, Sara Abou Rashed, 100–101

global connectedness, 87–90

Goodman & Owacki, 84

The Greatest Showman, 109

H

"happy place," 48

#HardWorkandDeterminationResults inGrowth hashtag, 24

Harwayne, Shelley, 97–98

hashtags
    #BelieveInArt, 95
    #BookBoss, 72
    #Digital4Good attitude, 107
    #DigitalCrew, 32
    #Feminist, 79
    #HardWorkandDetermination ResultsinGrowth, 24
    #ICANHELP, 40, 115, 117
    #IDIDHELP, 115
    #KeepAsking, 66
    #KeepLearning, 66
    #KidsCanTeachUs, 10, 65, 67, 76–78, 107
    #mapofmyself, 101
    #MyMalaysiaTeacher, 88
    #MyTaiwanTeacher, 88
    #SatSketch, 95, 124–126
    #SharkGuardian, 33
    #SocialJustice, 37
    #studentvoice, 112
    #TeachTheWorld, 13
    #TeamGenie, 64
    #whatsyourmap, 101

Have It All QR code, 77

heartbeeps, 16, 18

@HelentheShark, 33

hope, sparking, 102–106

Howard, Mary, 121

humanity, meaning of, 68

I

#ICANHELP hashtag, 40, 115, 117

ideas, connecting to digital experiences, 98. *See also* lesson ideas

#IDIDHELP hashtag, 115

"I'm not famous, I'm global!," 16, 23

innovation, 94

Innovative Designer Student Standard, 135

inspiration, finding in stories, 61–62

Instagram, 24

instructions, showing and telling, 127–130

international followers, 103

ISTE Educator Standards. *See also* teachers
    1: Learner, 17, 82
    2: Leader, 5, 47, 99
    3: Citizen, 29, 70
    4: Collaborator, 47
    5: Designer, 17
    6: Facilitator, 5, 29, 70, 99
    7: Analyst, 82

ISTE Standards for Students
    1: Empowered Learner, 127–130, 133–134
    2: Digital Citizen, 114–118, 120–130, 134
    3: Knowledge Constructor, 120–123, 134–135
    4: Innovative Designer, 135
    5: Computational Thinker, 135–136
    6: Creative Communicator, 114–118, 120–121, 124–130, 136
    7: Global Collaborator, 122–123, 136–137

J

Judge, Aaron, 116–117

K

Karr, Kim, 38–41

#KeepAsking hashtag, 66

#KeepLearning hashtag, 66

The KidLit Show, 56–60, 67

kids, understanding of technology, 3

Kids Can Teach Us: Te'Lario Watkins lesson idea, 122–123

#KidsCanTeachUs hashtag, 10, 65, 67, 76–78, 107

kidwatching, 84–85

Knowledge Constructor Student Standard, 120–123, 134–135

Your opinion matters:
Tell us how we're doing!

Your feedback helps ISTE create the best possible resources for teaching and learning in the digital age. Share your thoughts with the community or tell us how we're doing!

You can:

- Write a review at amazon.com or barnesandnoble.com.

- Mention this book on social media and follow ISTE on Twitter @iste, Facebook @ISTEconnects or Instagram @isteconnects

Email us at books@iste.org with your questions or comments.